TRAINS

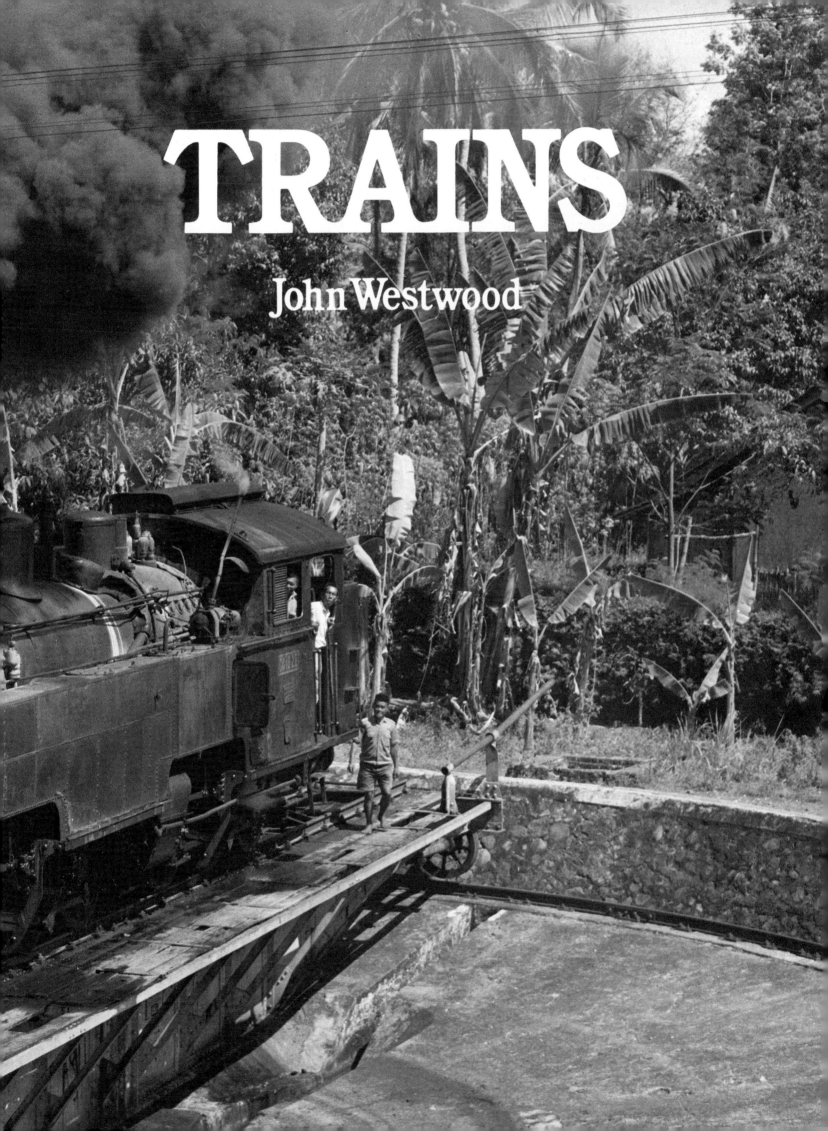

TRAINS

John Westwood

Contents

Jacket: A restored tank locomotive of the
Keighley and Worth Valley Railway in
Yorkshire.
Endpapers: A diesel-hauled British Railways
train crosses the Arthington Viaduct.
Title page: Britain's last main line steam
locomotive 'Evening Star' at York Station.
This page: An ore train on the Hammersley
Railway, Western Australia.

First published in 1978 by Octopus Books Limited
59 Grosvenor Street, London W1

© 1978 Octopus Books Limited

This edition first published in 1988

ISBN 1 55521 222 0

Printed in Hong Kong

The dawn of an era

In 1728 the wooden rails of a short wagon-way in northern England were replaced by cast iron rails. This date may be regarded as the start of the railway age. More iron railways soon appeared and by the end of the 18th century there were twenty such lines in Northumberland alone. Typically, these lines carried coal over the short distance between pithead and river wharf. They used gravity or horses to move the wagons, and were the exclusive property, and for the exclusive convenience, of the mining companies. That is, they were not 'common carriers', open to public traffic. The first common-carrier line was the Surrey Iron Railway (so called because its rails were of iron, not because iron was its traffic); this was opened near London in 1803, running from Wandsworth to Croydon. It was horse-drawn, and carried general freight for the public. Soon afterwards in 1807, the horse-drawn railway from Swansea to Oystermouth in south Wales became the first railway to carry fare-paying passengers.

The early wagonways found horse traction quite satisfactory until the Napoleonic wars raised the price of horses and fodder. It was this wartime inflation which prompted one of the English colliery lines, the Middleton Railway near Leeds, to change to steam traction. This happened in 1814, just ten years after the Cornishman Richard Trevithick had hauled a train of coal over the Penydaren Railway in south Wales, using a steam locomotive designed and built by himself. But even Trevithick, deservedly termed the 'father of the steam locomotive', only built upon the work of others. He had gained valuable experience when, as a mining engineer, he maintained and went on to improve steam pumping engines designed by James Watt. Trevithick would also have gained inspiration from the example of the French artillery officer Nicholas Cugnot, who built a steam road carriage in the 1760s. The carriage made short runs but, unfortunately for its inventor, it was hardly steerable. Trevithick's own early efforts in steam locomotion were road vehicles, and his one-cylinder railway locomotive was really only an improved version of his road carriage. The locomotive proved that steam traction was possible but it had a very short working life; like so many other locomotives, it caused too much damage to the flimsy plate-way on which it ran.

Trevithick's machine not only proved the feasibility of steam traction, but also showed that a smooth wheel running on a smooth metal track developed propulsive force without slipping. However, when the Middleton Railway decided to introduce steam traction it chose to use a cog system. Blenkinsop, the colliery's agent, decided that very light locomotives should be used so as to avoid track damage, and it was thought that they would have insufficient adhesion to prevent slipping if unaided by a cog mechanism. Blenkinsop employed a local Scottish engineer, Matthew Murray, to build the locomotives, which were strongly influenced by Trevithick's designs. They weighed only five tonnes and were mounted on four carrying wheels. The rack wheel was on one side of the locomotive and was powered by two cylinders. It provided the propulsive force by engaging in a row of rack teeth cast on the outside of one set of rails. The positioning of the rack at the side rather than in the centre left a path for the horses which were still used for some traffic. In practice, it was found that each of the four locomotives could do the work of sixteen horses, and far more cheaply. The line had many distinguished visitors, including the future Tsar Nicholas I, who would later authorize Russia's first railways. However, the rack system had a bleak future, partly because it was unnecessary except on very steep gradients and partly because the cogs tended to disengage at speeds above 8 km/h (5 mph).

Trevithick built only a handful of locomotives and they were more inventive than commercial. His early failures to interest a wide public led him to different ventures, and he died poor and unrecognized. How-

Left: The oldest locomotive still in existence, at rest in the Science Museum in London. 'Puffing Billy' was built in 1813 for the Wylam Colliery in northern England. It worked well, as did its sister engines, and conclusively proved that a smooth metal driving wheel could operate without slipping on a smooth metal rail.

ever, one Trevithick locomotive was acquired by the Wylam Colliery in Northumberland. It was too heavy for the track, and therefore little used. But its potential was acknowledged and in 1808 the colliery replaced its wooden rails with a cast-iron track, which in 1813 proved just strong enough to bear the weight of the colliery's new *Puffing Billy* series of locomotives. *Puffing Billy* and its consorts showed conclusively that a rack system was unnecessary. These locomotives, designed by the colliery's manager, William Hedley, had a vertical cylinder on each side of the boiler, driving a pivoting beam which was connected by a shaft and gear wheels with the driving wheels. To reduce the noise of the exhaust, Hedley led the used steam from the cylinders up a tall chimney where it created a draught for the fire. This blast-pipe effect provided a self-regulating mechanism whereby the heat produced by the fire varied in accordance with the amount of steam being used.

Not far from the Wylam Colliery was Killingworth Colliery, which was quick to note the success of its competitor's steam traction. George Stephenson, the Killingworth enginewright, had established a strong local reputation as a genius with engines, and he was entrusted with the design of a suitable locomotive. This appeared in 1814. Named *Blucher*, it was very similar to the Middleton Railway locomotives, although it employed no rack mechanism. However, *Wellington*, Stephenson's second locomotive, was a real advance, for the drive from the cylinders was taken via a connecting rod direct to the wheel, to which it was attached by a crank pin.

George Stephenson's employers owned several mines, which gave him great opportunities for locomotive building and, hence, locomotive improvement. He carefully educated his son Robert to make a suitable partner, and found financial backers. In 1825 Stephenson established Robert Stephenson & Company, the world's first company solely building locomotives. Meanwhile, thanks to his growing reputation, Stephenson had been appointed engineer of a much larger railway project, the Stockton and Darlington Railway. This line was built to take Durham coal mined near Darlington to the Tees estuary at Stockton. At the hilly, inland, end of the line, the trains were hauled by cables, but about 32 km (20 miles) of the line were operated by steam locomotives designed and built by the Stephensons. Apart from its length, this railway had many features of future main lines. It employed true rails, and rolling stock with flanged wheels; most previous lines had used L-shaped plates and flangeless wheels, less suitable for bearing heavy loads. (The superiority of the rail over the plate was improved when, in 1820, rails of rolled iron began to replace the more brittle cast iron in the building of new railways.) The Stockton and Darlington also established the so-called standard gauge, when Stephenson chose 4 ft 8 in (1422 mm) as the distance between the rails. Another half-inch was soon added, when it was discovered that

Left: One of the earliest American locomotive builders was the Norris Company, which first made its mark with this simple 4-2-0 design. The model shows one of the type built in Austria. Above: A model of a Great Western Railway locomotive of 1841, based on Stephenson's 'Patentee' type.

a looser fit between rail and wheel flange reduced friction without endangering safety.

The Stockton and Darlington was the first public steam railway. It was public in the sense not only of traffic (which was not confined to private coal traffic, and included passenger traffic) but also of finance, for capital was raised from the public. Finally, it was politically public, in that landowners whose opposition to the line could not be bought off by financial inducements were overcome by parliamentary process.

The Stockton and Darlington Railway's inaugural train ran in 1825. It was hauled by *Locomotion*, designed by George Stephenson and built by Robert Stephenson. However, colliery-type locomotives were not really adequate for long runs, especially as there were fewer stops during which steam pressure could be restored. In 1827 Stephenson's *Experiment* was built for the line. In this machine, boiler watertubes were placed in the flue, providing an extra heating surface. However, this idea, sound in theory, was not repeated because it complicated boiler maintenance.

Experiment was virtually George Stephenson's last initiative in locomotive design. Henceforth the Stephenson locomotive would be developed by Robert, while George concentrated on his grand strategy of covering Britain with a network of standard-gauge steam railways, preferably engineered by himself. Although he never achieved the monopoly of railway construction which he sought, a satisfying proportion of the earlier railways, both in Britain and

in Europe, were built under his guidance. Most notable among these was the Liverpool and Manchester Railway, which was the first inter-city steam railway and the first to be built with the aim of attracting traffic from other carriers. It was sponsored by businessmen who were dissatisfied with the service provided by the monopolistic Manchester to Liverpool canal.

Stephenson also had to master the opposition of those inside the new company who did not believe in steam locomotives and preferred to put their faith, and capital, in trains hauled by cables wound by stationary steam engines. However, Stephenson's friends within the company persuaded their colleagues to stage the Rainhill locomotive trials of 1829, in which competing designs of locomotives were set certain tasks to perform on a completed section of the company's line. The impressive performance of Robert Stephenson's *Rocket* at these trials was sufficient to assure locomotive haulage for the new line.

The Liverpool and Manchester Railway was opened by the Duke of Wellington in 1830. It quickly became a model for new railways elsewhere, for it was an immediate technical and commercial success. It was double-track, powered by locomotives which at the time were easily capable of hauling the required loads, and well managed. Right from the start it carried more traffic than had been anticipated even by the optimists, and, to the surprise of its directors, passenger traffic surpassed freight. Although freight traffic later became as important as passenger carrying, it was realized that the line was creating traffic with its fast, cheap, and regular services, in addition to attracting existing traffic away from less efficient and more expensive competitors, such as the canals.

The locomotives used by the Liverpool and

Far left: Stephenson's 'Locomotion' hauling the inaugural train of the Stockton and Darlington Railway in 1825. The roofed passenger vehicle was provided for the local dignitaries. The earliest railways provided ordinary passengers with simple benches mounted on what were essentially freight vehicles, and from these developed the wooden-seat four-wheel third class vehicle.
Above left and left: A late example of this type of vehicle is shown in the form used for many decades by the Dutch railways. Upper class passengers on early railways travelled in their own road carriages, which were loaded on to flat wagons. From this developed the more convenient first class railway carriage.
Above: A first class vehicle of the French Nord Railway clearly betrays the horse-carriage tradition embodied in these early rail vehicles.

Manchester were much better machines than the *Locomotion* of the Stockton and Darlington. In five years the Stephensons, and their competitors, had introduced several improvements. On the Stockton and Darlington the locomotive superintendent, Timothy Hackworth, was plagued with wheel and rail breakages and with locomotives which could not travel long distances without running short of steam. He therefore constructed locomotive wheels in sections, to give them flexibility, and he discovered that he could improve the draught on the fire by constricting the pipe which exhausted steam through the chimney. By thus increasing the velocity of the escaping steam Hackworth could create a white-hot blaze in the firebox. True, this blastpipe sucked large particles of unburned coal up the chimney, but then coal was cheap.

Another contribution to steam-raising capacity was the multitubular boiler, pioneered by the French engineer Marc Seguin. Previously, the hot fumes from the fire had been led to the chimney by a single large diameter flue. In the multitubular boiler they were passed through a number of smaller pipes instead. These pipes, or tubes, passed through the water in the boiler and thereby enabled a much larger proportion of the heat in the fumes to be transferred to the water.

The first practical use of the multitubular locomotive boiler was in the *Rocket*, the Stephensons' winning entry at the Rainhill trials. However, reliable construction and strict adherence to the rules were the main sources of the *Rocket*'s success, a success which led to *Rocket*-type locomotives being ordered for the Liverpool and Manchester. Robert Stephenson was already faced with the competition of other locomotive builders, and he introduced minor or major improvements with each new locomotive. From the 5-tonne, four-wheel *Rocket* was developed the 10-tonne *Planet* type, which had its cylinders in the subsequently conventional position beneath the chimney and horizontally in line with the wheels. Later came Stephenson's *Patentee*, which was equipped with a

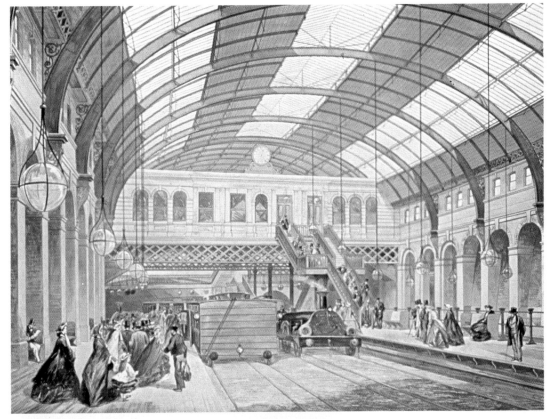

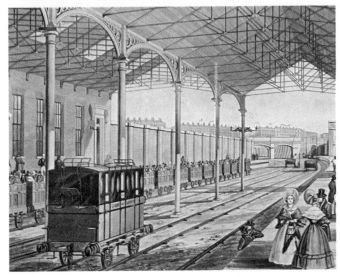

steam brake, and which had six wheels to spread the weight over rails which were still prone to failure.

The success of the Liverpool and Manchester Railway, and not least the dividends of over ten per cent which it habitually paid, gave a great boost to railway construction elsewhere. It is true that some lines had been started earlier, inspired, like the Liverpool and Manchester, by the success of the Stockton and Darlington. Among these were the St Etienne–Lyons Railway in France, engineered by the Seguins, the Canterbury and Whitstable in England, and the Baltimore and Ohio in the USA. As the more prosperous areas of Europe and America began to build lines, a major distinction arose between Britain and America on the one hand, and Continental Europe on the other. In the latter, governments drew up railway plans with the aim of building rational networks whereas in the Anglo-Saxon world free enterprise was given greater opportunity to determine where lines should be built. The result was that in Britain and America cities were often linked by several competing railways. At one time there were half a dozen different routes between New York and Chicago. The available traffic had to be shared out, and this excess capacity became a crushing burden in the 20th century. Such wasteful duplication was, however, largely avoided in continental Europe.

In America the government did later intervene to promote lines which private interests were unwilling to start. It did this by subsidies in the form of generous grants of land to companies building lines in un-developed areas. Most of the early lines were built to speed transit to the Atlantic ports. The Baltimore and Ohio was the first of these, with its initial section being opened in 1830. It was followed by the South Carolina Railroad from Charleston, the first American common carrier line to use steam traction on a daily basis. Although several locomotives were imported from England, American locomotive builders soon developed a style of their own, more suited to the cheaply laid tracks of the local railroads. Peter Cooper's one-tonne *Tom Thumb* impressed the directors of the Baltimore and Ohio in 1830, and the *Best Friend of Charleston*, the South Carolina's first locomotive, was built in New York. This locomotive's violent end, in a boiler explosion, was due to its fireman's discovery of the economy of labour which could result from holding down its safety valve.

13

Above: The 'American' type of locomotive had a four-wheel leading truck (or bogie) and four driving wheels. Admirably suited to the curving and lightly-laid American track, it was for decades the standard wheel arrangement

for both freight and passenger locomotives. The outside cylinders, almost universal in America, made it easier for the locomotive crew and the railways' mechanics to service this vulnerable part. This design was built around 1875.

Steam across North America

The early American railway companies tended to be smaller and poorer than their British counterparts. This was largely because they were sponsored by fairly small communities who were anxious to improve local commercial possibilities and had little thought of building up national or regional networks. Despite shortage of capital and frequent bankruptcies, these small companies rapidly enlarged the American railway route length. By 1843, using the lines of no fewer than nine companies which had end-on connections with each other, it was possible to travel from the Atlantic to the Great Lakes. But it was almost fifty years before it would be possible to travel from the Atlantic to the Great Lakes using the tracks of a single company. Most of the early lines connected the Atlantic seaboard with places inland, although the first railway in Texas, from Harrisburg, was opened in 1853, and the first Californian line, the Sacramento Valley Railroad, in 1856. The first big main line, the Pennsylvania Railroad's route from Philadelphia to Pittsburgh, was finished in 1854. Chicago had a nine-mile line as early as 1848, but it was another six years before Chicago had a through rail link with the eastern cities.

Largely because of the limited capital available, but partly because of a different philosophy, American railways were built inexpensively. Getting the lines built and the traffic moving was the first priority; upgrading the lines could be delayed until the traffic level both justified and paid for such improvement. Hence there were few of the expensive tunnels, cuttings, and embankments which typified British railways, and this meant that lines were more steeply graded and had sharper curves. As a result British-style locomotives and rolling stock were not really suitable for these more demanding conditions. Thus it was in America that the swivelling four-wheel truck, or bogie, first became a feature of locomotives and freight and passenger vehicles, enabling them to negotiate sharply curving track with safety and comfort. Tracks were laid, for the most part, directly on the ground. In due course many of the technical innovations adopted by American railroads were taken up in Europe and even Britain. Notable among these was the flat-bottom rail. Whereas the British, and British-influenced companies elsewhere, set their rails in cast-iron chairs which were then bolted to the wooden cross-ties, the Americans soon found it cheaper and easier to use a flat-bottomed rail, which could be spiked down directly. A century later, the British railways decided to change to flat-bottom rails.

Especially unmistakeable was the American school of locomotive design. Because it was easier to manufacture, the bar frame soon replaced the plate frame which was favoured in England. In this particular case, however, the impetus for change came from England for Edward Bury, a British competitor of the Stephensons in the locomotive-building business, exported some of his own bar-frame locomotives to the USA, where their advantages were soon realized. Swivelling leading trucks to ease locomotives around curves were devised by John Jervis of the Mohawk & Hudson Railroad as early as 1831. The Norris brothers, entrepreneurs more than inventors, combined the leading truck and the bar frame in a cheap design which was highly successful not only in America but in central Europe too, for the design was built also in Austria. British locomotive builders were highly disturbed when the Birmingham & Gloucester Railway ordered a batch of these machines. However, American locomotive builders never established a hold over the British or continental markets.

The American locomotives were extremely efficient. The Philadelphian Joseph Harrison was responsible for the 11-tonne *Gowan & Marx*, which in 1840 pulled unprecedented loads including, it was said, a train of 400 tonnes between Reading and Philadelphia at an average speed of 16 km/h (10 mph).

Because another cost-saving feature of American railroads was the absence of fencing, the locomotive bell (to warn humans), the cowcatcher or pilot (to prevent errant cattle derailing locomotives), and the headlight soon became features of American locomotives. An even more typical characteristic was the huge spark-arresting chimney, the 'bell-stack' or 'diamond stack', carried by most locomotives. Although in

Pennsylvania many locomotives burned anthracite, and later coal, wood was the typical fuel, and it was soon found that wood sparks, if unchecked at the chimney, could cause damaging woodland or prairie fires. The locomotive bell, which is still carried by American locomotives, soon proved insufficient and was supplemented by the whistle; this was especially suitable for giving early warning to citizens crossing the tracks at level crossings (grade crossings) which were much more common in America than in Britain, where bridges were favoured. The American locomotive was furnished with a cab, and usually a most commodious cab, long before such protection was regarded as a necessary part of the locomotive in Europe. Another feature was outside cylinders, much more accessible for attention than the inside cylinders favoured by British designers in the 19th century. Finally, the American locomotive builders soon established a lead in the size of locomotives.

The importance of railways on the national as opposed to the local level was emphasized by the Civil War. The public's imagination was fired by dramatic but unimportant events like 'The Great Locomotive Chase'. Meanwhile military and political

Top: Although built as late as 1913, this machine exhibits most of the characteristics of the early US locomotive: bar frames, wood fuel, spark-arresting chimney, commodious cab, outside cylinders, warning bell, and effective headlamp. Above: Wooden bodies, stove heating, and open end platforms were the marks of the North American railway passenger vehicle for most of the 19th century.

leaders were impressed by the railroads' ability to supply Sherman's army of 100,000 men over a single-track line passing over what was nominally enemy territory. In 1863 seven railroads, forced by war into unexpected coordination, succeeded in passing 23,000 federal troops 1900 km (1200 miles) from Virginia to Alabama in 14 days. Wartime coordination of railroads later led to the establishment of the American Association of Railroads, itself an offshoot of the 1872 conference of railroad leaders which at last standardized the time shown on the different lines' clocks and timetables. The Civil War also witnessed the introduction of steel rails in place of iron. It was the

Pennsylvania Railroad, faced with unprecedentedly heavy traffic on its main line, which first ordered these rails from England and which confirmed that not only did they wear out more slowly, but were less subject to dangerous breakages.

The Civil War, by impressing the potential of railroads on many previously indifferent minds, especially on military minds, gave a boost to the concept of a transcontinental railway. This would bind the isolated western territories to the union and thereby enhance the economic, political and military potential of the United States. Prompted by government subsidies in the form of land grants, the Union Pacific

Above: One of the 4–6–4 passenger locomotives used by the New York Central in the inter-war period. Its trailing four-wheel truck supported the huge firebox needed for sustained high power.

Railroad was formed to build westwards from the railhead at Omaha. The Central Pacific was formed at the same time to build eastwards over the Rockies to meet the former. In 1869 the two lines met in Utah, and the Pacific was linked to the Atlantic by a single line of rails and by accompanying telegraph line. The importance of this link was not merely in its effect on western development. Among other things, it inspired

further transcontinental railways, both in the USA and in Canada. It also finally settled the gauge question. Because of lack of centralized direction, American railways had been built to over twenty different gauges, although 4 ft 8½ in predominated. The transcontinental had been originally planned on the five-foot gauge, but the government changed this to 4 ft 8½ in and in so doing virtually standardized that gauge in the USA. Within a few years the 6 ft gauge of the Erie Railroad disappeared, as did the 4 ft 10 in of New Jersey, and the 5 ft 6 in and 5 ft gauge lines which existed elsewhere.

Along the tracks of the new transcontinentals there

Above: No 759, a Nickel Plate Railroad 2-8-4 now preserved. This is a typical example of the 'Super Power' locomotive developed by the Lima Locomotive Company. Top right: A 2-8-2 of the Illinois Central Railroad. Above right: A 2-8-0 of the Louisville and Nashville Railroad.

was a growing flow of westbound settlers, many of them immigrants attracted from Europe by the advertisements of the railroad companies. With their land grants, the railroads could offer not only cheap travel but also cheap land to prospective settlers, thus populating the regions they served and creating a future source of traffic. The enormous wheat and beef traffic moving to eastern markets was a subsequent, and expected, result of this policy. The Southern Pacific's New Orleans to Los Angeles line, and the Great Northern's and Northern Pacific's lines to Seattle, among others, were transcontinentals which contributed to, and then shared, the new western prosperity.

These examples were not unnoticed in Canada, which at that time consisted of a collection of British colonies which the London government wished to unite in a federation. British Columbia was the most isolated of these colonies, and seemed to be in danger

of succumbing to American influence. The idea of a transcontinental railway to link the newer western colonies with the older settlements of Ontario and Quebec seemed to offer not only a connecting link between colonies but also an inducement to persuade a reluctant British Columbia to join the proposed federation. Despite the difficult terrain of the Rockies and some financial problems, the strong political support in Canada and Britain, the capital resources of London, and the energy of the American contractor van Horne enabled the new Canadian Pacific Railway to run its first train to the Pacific in 1886. The

inaugural train took 139 hours to move from Montreal to Vancouver, which at the time seemed miraculously fast. The success of Canadian Pacific persuaded the Russian government to built its Trans-Siberian line to bind Russia's far eastern possessions more securely to its empire.

By mid-century the North American passenger car had taken, more or less, its final shape; future changes would be in size and materials rather than in layout. It had open platforms at each end, across which passengers entered and left the vehicle. These platforms also could serve as rudimentary shock absorbers in collisions. There was a central aisle, with seats on either side of the car; the European compartmented car was not favoured. Toilets were provided at each end, and lighting was by candle or oil lamp. The bodies were of wood, and the main developments after 1850 were increasing ornamentation, a gradual increase of the original 12 metre (40 ft) length and, for

the better trains, replacement of plain wood by plush covered seats. Four-wheel trucks at each end assured a fairly steady ride over uneven track.

After the Civil War the Pullman car was provided by many railroads for their better-off customers. These cars were furnished and staffed by George Pullman's company and provided passengers with sleeping accommodation, mainly in the form of pull-down bunks. A sleeping car supplement was collected by Pullman, while the operating railroad benefited by the first-class ticket which sleeper passengers were required to buy. Pullman had many rivals, but emerged triumphant from the competition and the Pullman car became an important feature of the best long-distance trains. Indeed, some trains later consisted of Pullman cars only, with no space for the sitting 'coach' passenger. Passenger train speeds were not high, despite the hot competition between different railroads. The track and the locomotives were not really adequate for reliable and safe high-speed running, which did not appear until the end of the century. In the 1870s, for example, it took 30 hours to travel from New York to Chicago, but in subsequent decades this was progressively reduced to less than 16 hours.

Freight cars, too, soon acquired the forms which were to persist until the present day. Like passenger vehicles, and for the same reason, they were soon mounted on two four-wheel trucks; the European-style freight car with its rigid two-axle wheelbase was quite unsuitable. The covered van-type vehicle, known as the box-car, became the standard general purpose vehicle and was (and is) used for traffic which in other countries would be carried by specialized

vehicles; even grain and timber are still carried in this type of car at times of heavy traffic. The tail-end vehicle of the American freight train, the 'caboose' in which the conductor lived, slept, and ate while pursuing his duties, was well established in the 1860s. High casualties among railway staff were caused by the inadequate couplings and brakes of that period. Although chains were soon replaced by link-and-pin couplings, the latter were not always safe to handle and moreover broke quite frequently. But in the 1860s a succession of American inventors developed an automatic coupler of the jaw type. This was not only stronger, permitting heavier trains, but because the jaws locked automatically when one car was brought into contact with another, it eliminated the perilous

job of manual coupling. Soon afterwards the braking problem was largely solved by George Westinghouse. Hitherto trains had been stopped by brakemen climbing along the roofs of the train and screwing down the handbrakes on a proportion of the vehicles, a dangerous and not always effective job. Westinghouse's brake used compressed air cylinders, operated from and by the locomotive, to operate brakes continuously down the train; locomotive men, by releasing air from the brake cylinders, could apply the brakes instantly and with whatever degree of urgency

they required. However, many railroads refused to spend money on Westinghouse's brake until forced to do so by public opinion acting through Congress.

In fact, although the quarter-century preceding World War 1 is often regarded as the golden age of American railroading, railroad administrations of the time would have scoffed at this idea. They found themselves increasingly shackled by state and government regulations, the fruit of public hostility which had been growing more intense over the decades. To an extent this hostility was justified. The railways were America's first big business, and many of them had taken full advantage of the benefits which size and power had given them. The public was conscious that 'railway kings' like Vanderbilt might have built up big

Below: The Canadian Pacific Railway was one of the few North American companies to build its own locomotives. This 'Royal Hudson' type passenger engine was built in the 1930s.

systems like the New York Central from a host of smaller weak lines, and in so doing benefited the economy, but they also knew that such men had plundered railroad shareholders in the process, had sponsored lines intended not so much to serve necessary transportation needs as to embarrass competing lines, and had used their monopoly powers to levy unfair passenger and freight rates. They knew, too, and the episode with Westinghouse's brake and countless fatal accidents had emphasized this, that the rail-

roads were not very keen to spend money on safety measures. All this encouraged increasing government intervention in the management of the railways; the Interstate Commerce Commission was established to regulate railroad rates, railroad building, railroad stock transactions, and railroad safety. At first such intervention was beneficial, but by the middle of the 20th century it prevented those railroads which had competent managements from taking effective action to maintain profitability in the face of competition

Left: Although it was the
crack streamliners which
received all the publicity,
the majority of American
passenger trains in the
last decades of steam
resembled the one shown
in this picture, taken in
1952. It is a Milwaukee
Railroad train, hauled by
a typical American 4–6–2,
leaving the old Milwaukee
station in Chicago. The
grade crossing over a busy
street was, and is, typical
of American practice, and
the locomotive's bell can
be seen swinging as it
warns of the train's
approach. The heavy
passenger car, in which
wood is still an important
component, is very
different from the
all-metal, air-conditioned,
reclining-seat vehicles
which were running in the
more-publicised trains of
the period. The
unembellished black paint
of the locomotive, cheaper
to apply and maintain,
was typical of the period
and in contrast to the
bright colours of the new
diesel locomotives.

from the airways, highways, and shipping routes.

The so-called golden age of American railroads witnessed the formation of large railway systems by the amalgamation of smaller lines; this was achieved not by government action but by share dealings arranged at first by the railway 'kings', and later by more responsible investment bankers. There was also a spate of new, expensively-built and often unnecessary lines. California received a new link with the east when the Western Pacific Railroad was built to

San Francisco in 1909. For purely competitive reasons yet another main line, the Milwaukee Railroad, was built to Seattle. The Florida East Coast Railroad was extended over the sea for 170 km (107 miles) to Key West over a succession of trestles, islands and embankments.

Locomotives were steadily becoming bigger and heavier. The old faithful 4–4–0 was replaced first by the 2–6–0 and 4–6–0 and 2–8–0, and then by the Pacific (4–6–2) for passenger service and the Mikado

(2–8–2) for freight. However, the fastest-ever engine was reputed to be No 999 of the New York Central, designed by the Scotsman William Buchanan, which was said to have reached 180 km/h (112 mph) in 1893. In 1908 appeared the 2–10–2 type, an advance on the 2–8–2, and in 1912 the 4–8–2 type, an advance on the 4–6–2. There was a definite predilection for a trailing pair of wheels to support a firebox which was considerably larger than that of contemporary European engines. This ample firebox was required not so much because of inferior coal but to provide the steam-raising capacity needed to haul very heavy trains over stiffly graded tracks. Huge firegrates were often too much for one fireman, and the first successful mechanical stoker appeared in 1905. In general, American locomotives were less economical on coal than European, were much more heavy and powerful, and could survive rough maintenance more successfully. There was no attempt to conceal their working parts, and although to European eyes this made them seem untidily dressed, they were consequently easier to maintain.

The need for better public relations was one reason why around the turn of the century American railroads began to operate faster and more luxurious passenger trains. Passenger revenues were much less important than freight, and it is doubtful whether the more celebrated trains even returned the money that was invested in them, but in the heyday of the popular press they were a fine way of obtaining favourable publicity. The competition between the New York Central's *Twentieth Century Limited* and the Pennsylvannia's *Broadway Limited* on the overnight New York to Chicago run enhanced the prestige

Above: Short lines once proliferated in the USA, and one of their favourite locomotive types was the 2–6–0, one of which is shown here at Blanca, Colorado. Above right: In the last decade of steam traction, steam locomotives like this 4–8–4, built for heavy mainline service, were often employed on local duties. Below right: A Union Pacific 2–8–2 with an obviously unprofitable mixed train in Colorado.

of both companies. By 1905 the New York–Chicago schedule had been brought down to 18 hours, compared to the 25 hours of the 1880s. Similarly competitive services were operated on other routes, especially by the companies struggling for the transcontinental traffic.

Train speeds were increasing; the *Twentieth Century Limited*, for example, averaged 77 km/h (48 mph). Passenger comfort, and safety, also improved. The open platform of the traditional passenger car had, in the 1890s, been enclosed to form a sheltered vestibule, which also enabled passengers to move safely from one vehicle to another. After 1905 the all-steel car, much safer in collision and fire than the wooden car, came into general use. In the 1880s the old heating stoves were replaced by radiators supplied with hot steam from the locomotive, and the dangerous oil lamps were at the same time replaced by the European-style Pintsch gas lamp. (Electric lighting, first introduced in Britain, also appeared on some crack trains in the late 1880s). Passenger cars became longer and heavier. It was believed that heavier cars ran more steadily and it was not long before passenger vehicles appeared with six-wheel in place of four-wheel trucks. It was not until lightweight streamlined trains appeared in the thirties that this trend was reversed.

Freight train progress was less marked. It was the era of the 'drag freight'; cars were held in yards until sufficient were assembled to make what was considered a fitting load for the new powerful locomotives. With a virtual monopoly of freight movement, the railroads could afford long transit delays in yards and the operation of ultra-slow freight trains. Before World War 1 the average speed of freight trains was well below 16 km/h (10 mph).

The great days of the steam-hauled train were the inter-war years, when steam locomotive designers were faced both with the competition of new forms of transport and of new forms of motive power, notably electric and diesel locomotives. Huge Mallet-type articulated locomotives were built, mainly for freight. Most high-speed passenger services were entrusted to 4–6–4, 4–6–2, 4–8–4 and 4–8–2 locomotives. With the advent of streamlined diesel trains, a number of steam locomotives were also streamlined, more for the sake of public relations than for the doubtful technical advantages of reducing frontal air resistance. Because of highway competition, faster freight trains were

needed, and a new generation of freight locomotives was built. The Lima Locomotive Company pioneered the use of the four-wheel truck beneath the firebox with its new 2–8–4 and 2–10–4 designs. These were a result of the realization that it was not tractive effort, but horsepower, that determined a locomotive's capacity. With their huge fireboxes these locomotives could sustain high horsepower outputs for mile after mile.

After World War II the diesel-electric locomotive steadily ousted the steam machine. The coal-hauling Norfolk and Western, together with the two Canadian transcontinentals, the Canadian National and Canadian Pacific, were the last strongholds of steam haulage, but by 1961 mainline steam had disappeared in North America.

Below left: Most successful and longest-lived of the spate of narrow-gauge lines built in the 1870s and 1880s, the Denver and Rio Grande's 914 mm (3 ft) gauge Colorado lines survived as freight carriers until after World War II. A section is still used as a tourist line.
Below: An early Mallet 2–6–6–2 design freight locomotive built by Baldwin.

The steam age in Europe

Railway development was rapid in Britain and continental Europe after the opening of the Liverpool and Manchester Railway in 1830. In western Europe the key lines were in service by mid-century, and by 1875 the mainline networks were largely complete, although gaps remained to be filled. Progress was, however, uneven. Some countries, most noticeably Russia, lagged behind; indeed the great age for Russian railway building was the 1890s. But the pace of railway growth varied greatly from year to year, depending usually on the availability of capital. Even in Britain, where the Industrial Revolution was already creating new wealth, capital investment was very variable. During periods like the 'Railway Mania' of 1846 those with savings were so anxious to invest

their resources in railway shares that too many lines were started (272 Railway Acts were passed in 1846), and railway bankruptcies ruined thousands of families. Such catastrophes in turn aroused distrust so that, for a time, savers preferred to invest funds elsewhere.

Among the earliest and most important British lines were the London and Birmingham, finished in 1838, which by means of the neighbouring Grand Junction Railway connected with the Liverpool and

Below: This inside-cylinder passenger 4–4–0 was built in 1901 for the South Eastern & Chatham Railway. Right: A 2–6–4 tank locomotive, with the rear four-wheel truck supporting the coal bunker. Below right: 'Henry Oakley', a 4–4–2 passenger locomotive of Britain's Great Northern Railway.

Manchester; these three companies soon joined to form the so-called 'Premier Line', the London and North Western Railway. What would later become the most celebrated of the British companies, the Great Western Railway, dated from the same period. It was always a very individualistic enterprise. Engineered by Brunel, it scorned Stephenson's standard gauge of 1435 mm (4 ft 8½ in) in favour of a broad gauge of 2140 mm (7 ft ¼ in), and it was not long before the gauge question became the burning issue of British railway politics. Eventually parliament decided that 4 ft 8½ in should become the standard gauge, and the last broad gauge train from London to the west pulled out of the capital in 1892.

By 1870 Britain had 24,500 km (15,250 miles) of railway, and was still ahead of other European countries. Her main lines were virtually finished, although the last and rather unnecessary main line, that of the Great Central Railway from south Yorkshire to London, was built only in 1899. Although new railway lines could only be started with the passage of a parliamentary bill, parliament had rarely limited the proliferation of unnecessary lines. Competition was considered healthy, so many cities were connected by several different companies, all competing for traffic. Among the routes on which com-

31

petition was hottest were those from London to Scotland where two consortia of companies known as the east coast and west coast routes tried to outmatch each other in speed and service; the London–Plymouth service, where the Great Western and South Western companies battled for the prestigious but not especially lucrative Atlantic liner traffic and whose increasingly high speeds culminated in a fatal derailment on Salisbury curve; and the sterile and vicious battle between two companies for the Kent traffic, the most obvious feature of which was a few superb services to catch the public eye, and mediocrity elsewhere.

Railway building was organized very differently in continental Europe. There, governments tried to avoid wasting resources on lines which did not really further the economic development of their territories, and at the same time they tried to ensure that the new railway monopolies would not make excessive profits. Belgium was the first nation to initiate a rational plan of railway construction, with two lines traversing the country and crossing almost at right angles, the main depots and workshops being situated at the central junction.

Not all governments found railway building so easy. They could draw up plans, but this did not always bring forth the required private capital. A solution to this problem was first advanced by the King of Holland, who guaranteed prospective investors that if the lines they financed were unprofitable he would personally pay them an annual dividend from his own resources. Thus was born the 'guarantee system' which offered a risk-free incentive to private capital. Often the guarantee was so generous as to constitute virtually a licence to print money, but it certainly enabled railway construction to go ahead rapidly.

The guarantee system, with other incentives, was widely employed in France and Russia. The first French railway plan of 1842 was perhaps the most clear cut of all, and its effects are still visible. It envisaged not so much a network as a spider's web of lines, all radiating from Paris. Only in later years were a few peripheral lines built and these never provided services comparable with '*les grandes lignes*' starting from Paris. In Germany and Italy the French type of centralization was avoided because at the beginning of the railway age these nations were still divided into several states, each with its own railway ambitions. However, with the growing dominance of Prussia, by the end of the century Berlin had become a centre of converging railway lines. In Russia the tsars had insisted on a rational plan of construction. The first

Right: The 'single', a locomotive with a single pair of driving wheels, was used by many British companies for their fastest trains in the 19th century. This example was built for Scotland's Caledonian Railway.

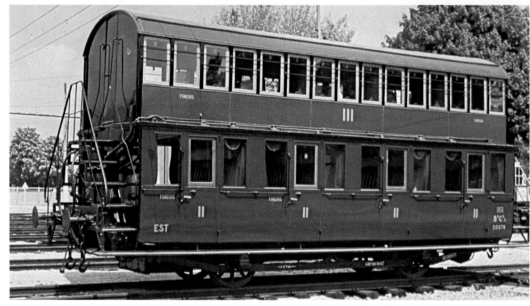

Above: A Chapelon compound Pacific of French National Railways at Boulogne Maritime. Chapelon's double chimney, the outward sign of his improved draughting, is clearly visible.
Right: A double-deck vehicle of France's Est Railway. Several continental railways distinguished the three passenger classes by paint of different colours. Far right: Another Chapelon locomotive, a 2–8–2 built in the 1940s, at Le Mans locomotive depot.

main line linked the old and new capitals of Moscow and St Petersburg. This railway, built to very high standards under the supervision of an American engineer and Russian army officers, was followed by lines from St Petersburg to Warsaw, and from Moscow to the south. The Trans-Siberian came in the 1890s. Like many other Russian lines, it was built as much for military reasons as for economic. The Russian government always had difficulty in raising capital and was largely dependent on foreign, especially French, investors.

Another empire with railway ambitions was the Austro–Hungarian. Relying for finance and advice on the great new banking houses like the Rothschilds and Pereires, the Vienna government regarded the railway as important not only for channelling international trade to its own Adriatic ports, but also as a means of binding its heterogeneous collection of nations into

something more resembling a union. In this it was ultimately unsuccessful; when the Empire broke up after World War 1 its railway system was broken up between the new nation states of central and southern Europe. Switzerland, a less pretentious collection of nations, had more modest goals for its railways. Financed largely by French banks, the early main lines were not very profitable, but after the great Alpine tunnels were bored the Swiss railways obtained a lucrative share of the international traffic to the Mediterranean. Elsewhere in Europe, Spain was distinguished by the choice of a broad gauge (1676 mm or 5 ft 6 in) for a railway system which, because of the sparse and impoverished population, seemed unlikely ever to prove profitable.

From about the 1870s many governments discovered that resources were lacking to build the network of secondary lines which were considered necessary. The

cheaper narrow gauge was therefore adopted for some new lines, especially in France where metre-gauge secondary railways were built with the participation of local governments. In Belgium a separate administration for secondary lines was set up, and in Switzerland many communities built their own metre-gauge lines. Narrow-gauge lines also became popular in parts of Germany, especially Saxony, and in Russia and Portugal. They were not very widespread in Britain, although it had been the technical success of the Ffestiniog Railway in Wales which had inspired many of the European narrow-gauge projects.

Almost all railways made more revenue from freight than from passengers, the notable exception being in Holland, where most freight continued to be carried by the canals. However, it was passenger services which most interested the general public and which established a railway's reputation. In Britain, the rudimentary passenger accommodation of the Liverpool and Manchester Railway was soon improved upon. The first advance, made on that railway, was the replacement of loose chain couplings with screw couplings, so that trains could start with less of a jerk. In course of time the open wagons with wooden benches which carried the third class passenger were roofed over. British railways had not at first been favourably inclined towards the low-fare third class passenger, but Gladstone's Railway Bill of 1844 obliged each company to provide at least one low-fare daily train over their routes. Eventually managements discovered that the third class passenger, because of

his numbers and because his vehicles were well-filled, was much more lucrative than the other classes. In 1870, the Midland Railway recognized this by providing him with padded seats and faster trains, an example which competition forced other companies to imitate.

In Britain, as in Europe generally, the compartmented passenger vehicle was favoured. The centre-aisle open passenger car as used in America was encountered only occasionally. Passengers probably preferred the sense of privacy which this conferred; it was possible, for example, for a single family to reserve a compartment for itself. When the side corridor was introduced for the longer-distance trains it was just as easy as in America for toilets to be provided at the ends of the vehicles.

In the 1870s the Belgian Nagelmackers introduced his sleeping cars (*wagons-lit*) to European railways. Nagelmackers' company, the future International Sleeping Car Company (which still provides its familiar blue sleeping cars for international services), furnished and staffed the cars, which were attached to selected trains. In 1883 Nagelmackers succeeded in launching the first of 'The Great International Trains'. This was the *Orient Express*, which ran from Paris through central Europe to Turkey, its passengers enjoying the comfort of sleeping and dining cars. Other railway administrations soon accepted Nagelmackers' further proposals, and by 1914 Europe was criss-crossed by a network of long-distance sleeping car services. Even the Trans-Siberian Railway had a wagons-lit train, carrying the name of the company all the way across Asia to the Pacific.

At the other end of the social scale, hordes of new passengers made use of short-distance, low-fare services provided around the cities. This began what was virtually a population transfer, as workers discovered that they could with little inconvenience live further away from their place of employment. Thus did the railways create suburbs, and at the same time an immense suburban traffic which in later years they would regret, because after a few decades it was found that the low fares did not cover the high costs of heavy peak-hour traffic. In some cities of continental Europe, to avoid lengthening stations to accommodate longer suburban trains, double-deck cars were introduced. However, British railways, whose height and width clearances were more restricted, could hardly adopt this expedient, and in consequence a four-track railway was often needed to accommodate the peak-hour traffic.

By the mid-19th century the steam locomotive had reached its more or less final form. Future improvements were limited to details. It is a rather remarkable fact that right up to the end of the steam era the locomotive included vital components which were inherently unreliable. For example, the injector, which fed boilers with fresh water, often failed in service, which was why most locomotives carried two. The amount of water in the boiler was indicated by a frail glass cylinder, liable to burst. The leaking boiler tube was a problem never completely solved. Speedometers were regarded as a luxury; in Britain right until the end of steam only passenger locomotives carried them, even though it was equally important for freight trains to observe speed limits. Meanwhile, while such basic faults remained unremedied, locomotive designers strove to increase the power of their locomotives without imposing too much extra weight and stress on the track, and at the same time tried to gratify their boards of directors by designing locomotives which would produce more work for less coal.

Around the turn of the century the steady progress in the size of what were really conventional locomotives was enlivened by new departures. The articulated locomotive (described in a later chapter) was developed in several forms and enabled much larger locomotives to be accommodated on existing track. Meanwhile the quest for fuel economy brought the compound system, in which used steam leaving the cylinder was not exhausted directly through the blastpipe and chimney, but gave up a further part of its energy in another, low-pressure, cylinder. Many permutations of high- and low-pressure cylinder were tried, with varying success. French railways were the

Right: Although Switzerland once had a thriving steam locomotive industry, electric traction was adopted early. These two 2–8–0 locomotives are operated by the metre-gauge Rhaetian Railway only for excursions.

Left: 'Sir Nigel Gresley', a streamlined Pacific named after its designer, and a sister of the record-breaking 'Mallard', working an excursion train. Above: One of the better-known international trains, the 'Direct Orient Express', in Yugoslavia, hauled by a German-built locomotive. Below right: An early dining car, that of the 'Orient Express'.

most enthusiastic users of compound locomotives, but most of the British and German railways considered that the extra building and maintenance expense was greater than the fuel saving. Much depended, obviously, on the local price of coal. In the early 20th century Schmidt of the Prussian State Railways developed his steam superheater, which brought most of the thermal advantage of compounding at a lower expense. The superheater was an arrangement of pipes which led steam on its way to the cylinders through a chamber containing hot gases escaping from the fire box. This additionally raised the temperature of the steam and made it less liable to condense in the cylinders. The thermal efficiency of the steam locomotive was notoriously low (it converted only about 5–6 per cent of the fuel's potential energy into useful work), and Schmidt's work raised this coefficient by one or two per cent.

In many countries World War 1 brought significant changes in railway policies. For many decades a burning political question had been railway nationalization. Railways, it was said, were too important to be left to profit-making individuals. Some countries had state-owned railways from the start, but most

began with private enterprises and then experimented with total or partial state ownership. In the war the belligerents had placed their railways under central direction, and this had worked well, with the railways carrying unprecedentedly large flows of traffic, often in totally new directions. In Britain the coordination of the various railway companies, with its elimination of the previously wasteful competition, had made such an impression that a return to the old order was unwelcome. But instead of nationalization there was amalgamation, with the multitude of old companies merged into just four large private companies: an enlarged Great Western Railway and the new Southern, London Midland and Scottish, and London and North Eastern railways. In Germany the collapse of the empire led directly to the formation of the *Reichsbahn*, a state corporation managing the nationwide railway network. Hitherto, the German states had administered their own railway systems, although towards the end the predominance of Prussia had brought a certain standardization of policies and practices. In France a national railway company, the Etat, had been established before World War 1 to take over certain impecunious lines in south western France. For the time being the Etat coexisted with the private companies but in 1938 French National Railways (SNCF) was established. In Britain nationalization followed World War II, British Railways being established in 1948.

In Britain and western Europe the inter-war years witnessed the heyday of fast steam train operation. The importance of good public relations, the existence of growing competition from the private automobile, and the fashion for streamlining, combined with a new generation of talented locomotive designers to result in such trains as the Great Western's *Cheltenham Flyer*, the LMS *Royal Scot* and the LNER's *Flying Scotsman* and *Silver Jubilee* successively breaking records for top speed or fastest schedules. Between London and Edinburgh, non-stop runs became possible with the corridor locomotive tender, enabling crews to be changed en route (British locomotives had long had the capacity to scoop up water from track troughs at speed). On the continent, because there was little direct competition between railways, the high-speed train was less prominent, but there was much progress in locomotive performance to interest the newspaper-reading public. In France the engineer André Chapelon brought the compound locomotive to an unprecedented peak of efficiency and performance, largely by means of scientifically designed exhaust and draughting arrangements, careful design of steam passages, and full exploitation of high-temperature superheating. In Germany, where trains like the *Flying Hamburger* were showing the potentialities of diesel traction, the locomotive designers, after first having introduced for the *Reichsbahn* a range of standard locomotives based on Prussian practice, turned their attention to high-speed locomotives. A streamlined 4–6–4 locomotive built by Borsig reached a speed of 200 km/h (124 mph) on trial with a train over level track. However, the official speed record for steam traction was finally broken by *Mallard* of the London and North Eastern Railway. In 1938 this streamlined 4–6–2 locomotive designed by Nigel Gresley reached 203 km/h (126 mph) with a train on a descending gradient.

The outbreak of World War II marked the end of the high-speed steam era, but also a beginning of a new and final period of achievement as wartime placed unexpected tasks on the railways. In Britain the locomotives of Nigel Gresley, designed for hauling trains of around eight or ten cars, found themselves hauling troop trains of 18 or even 24 vehicles. After the liberation of France some of Chapelon's highly sophisticated passenger locomotives were used to move 2000-tonne trains of desperately needed coal to the Paris region. In Germany several thousand 2–10–0 wartime standard locomotives were built. These *Kriegslok* units were used by the German army and all over German-occupied Europe. Because of their usefulness and also because of their sheer weight of numbers, it is perhaps not surprising that some of these last examples of the Prussian design school are still at work in central Europe.

Difficult post-war conditions and the need for post-war reconstruction, combined with the inter-war advances in electric and diesel traction, meant that the steam locomotive's days were numbered after 1945. The war-ravaged Dutch railways soon abandoned steam (Switzerland, with its abundant hydroelectricity, had long since opted for an electric system). Here and there the steam locomotive enjoyed an Indian summer. A Chapelon locomotive under trial produced such impressive power and efficiency statistics that the electric locomotive designers had, literally, to return to their drawing boards. In Britain the pre-war *Castle* and *King* 4–6–0s of the Great Western, and the Pacifics of the other three companies, were employed on the best trains until the 1960s, and indeed steam locomotive construction continued until the mid-1950s. In the German Democratic Republic the fast Berlin–Dresden trains were still in 1977 hauled by 4–6–2s first built in the 1920s as part of the *Reichsbahn*'s standardization policy. But, all the time and at varying rates in different countries, the diesel and electric locomotive was slowly squeezing out its cheaper but less efficient predecessor.

Steam in Asia and Australasia

India, with China, seems destined to be the last stronghold of the steam locomotive. Indian railways were built by the British, and their locomotives were plainly of British origin; apart from the difference in gauge, the provision of headlights and cowcatchers, and of roomy cabs with slatted shutters, the Indian locomotive would not have seemed out of place in a British station. Passenger rolling stock varied from the first-class compartments equipped with berths and dining table, through second and 'intermediate' class, to the third class used by the masses. At times third-class accommodation was horrifyingly crowded and insanitary, but the fares were very low. The slowness and assorted horrors of third-class travel were one of the favourite debating points of Indian nationalists during the struggle for independence, and after India became a separate nation one of the first tasks of Indian Railways was to provide fast 'Janata' trains of comfortable third-class rolling stock. At the same time, however, it did not neglect to introduce a new very superior class, air-conditioned, for the use of top people.

The soundly-engineered and dense railway network was one of Britain's most valuable legacies to the new India. Part of that legacy, however, was a gauge problem. As elsewhere, it had been found that after the main lines were complete there were localities which still needed a railway but which could not really originate enough traffic to make a line profitable. Capital was in any case limited, despite the guarantee system used by the Indian government to attract capital from London. This problem was especially urgent because India was a land of local but deadly famines, and railways seemed an excellent way of making sure that food was distributed where it was most needed. For this reason a secondary network of metre-gauge lines was built to supplement the 1676 mm (5 ft 6 in) gauge main lines. The use of a narrower gauge, by reducing costs, certainly enabled more lines to be built, but the need to tranship passengers and freight at break-of-gauge stations is expensive and inconvenient. The problem was aggravated when it was decided to permit even narrower gauges (610 mm and 750 mm or 2 ft and 2 ft 6 in) for short lines of local significance. Thus when India became independent in 1947 her railway mileage was divided between four gauges, with the broad and metre gauges predominating and approximately equal in extent. Since then some metre gauge mileage has been converted to broad gauge, but the problem is still far from solved.

After Independence the British helped the Indians to establish the Chitaranjan Locomotive Works. The main output of this works consisted of the new WG class of 2–8–2 locomotives, mainly for freight, and of a bullet-nosed 4–6–2 for passenger service, the WP class. On the metre gauge new classes of 4–6–2 and 2–8–2 also made their appearance. These four classes now handle most of the mainline traffic still operated by steam traction.

Although electrification and dieselization have ousted steam traction from many of the best-known trains, such as the *Grand Trunk Express* from Delhi to Madras and the *Punjab Mail* from Bombay to Delhi, there are still many named broad-gauge and metre-gauge trains in the charge of modern Pacifics. To foreign visitors the best-known steam train is the broad-gauge *Taj Express*, specially designed to whisk visitors on a day-trip from Delhi to Agra. Unlike most Indian named trains, this does not provide sleeping accommodation, as the distance is only 195 km (121 miles) which the WP covers in 185 minutes.

In another part of the British Empire, Australia, railways were organized very differently from the Indian railways. The early railways, built inland from scattered ports, were sponsored by the individual colonies and were not regarded as forming part of a future all-Australian network. Victoria was first, with its line from Melbourne to Port Melbourne in 1854. This was followed by the Sydney to Paramatta line

Above left: The 38 class Pacific, built in the 1950s for the New South Wales Government Railways, was of purely Australian design and construction and a most handsome and successful type. Left: Another view of a class 38 locomotive, one of several painted green.

built by the New South Wales colony in 1855, and South Australia's Adelaide to Port Adelaide line in 1856. Each colony chose its own gauge, with the result that Australia soon had, and continues to have, a gauge problem. This was not really the fault of the London government which, still involved in its own British 'battle of the gauges', did its best to ensure that the neighbouring colonies of New South Wales, Victoria and South Australia should have a standard gauge. But in the end, local inertia, confusion, and personal animosity caused New South Wales to opt for 1435 mm (4 ft 8½ in) and Victoria and South Australia for 1600 mm (5 ft 3 in). South Australia later confused the question further by building 1067 mm (3 ft 6 in) gauge lines in outlying areas, while the colonies of Western Australia, Queensland, and Tasmania chose 1067 mm (3 ft 6 in), as their mainline standard. Soon after the formation of the Australian confederation the new central government in Canberra undertook the Trans Australian Railway to link the east with Perth and Western Australia. By choosing the 4 ft 8½ in gauge for this transcontinental route, Canberra effectively

nominated that gauge as the future standard. However, changing the gauge of the lines outside New South Wales was expensive, and has been undertaken very slowly. A first important step was the continuation of the New South Wales Government Railway's east coast main line into Brisbane, thus bringing the standard gauge into Queensland. Later, a new standard gauge line in Victoria to the border with New South Wales made possible the through running of trains between Sydney and Melbourne. More recently, new standard gauge lines have extended the transcontinental standard gauge to New South Wales and across Western Australia, making it possible to run trains from Sydney to Perth.

Australian railways tended to follow British practice. Most locomotives were imported from England, although most of the states did build some units in their own local workshops. Thus for the most part the Australian locomotive was clearly a product of the British school of design. But there were some exceptions. In the 1920s an americanizing management of the South Australian Railways decided to buy

American-style locomotives but these, paradoxically, were ordered from Britain. Later, the New South Wales Government Railways introduced locomotives of its own design, whose style suggested that a native Australian school was in the making. The most notable of these types was the class 38 Pacific.

Freight and passenger cars also reflected British design. The compartmented passenger vehicle was common, although externally there were American features. Many passenger cars had open end platforms, and a series of heavy vehicles built for the joint Victorian and South Australian 'Overland' service between Adelaide and Melbourne was distinctly American in appearance. Train speeds were not high by European standards, but most railways operated one or two crack trains whose main appeal was comfort rather than speed. Such trains included the Victorian Railway's *Spirit of Progress*, from Melbourne to the New South Wales border, the Western Australian *Australind*, which in the late 1940s covered the 185 km (115 miles) from Perth to Bunbury in 3 hrs 15 min behind a post-war Pacific locomotive, and the *Sunshine Express* of the Queensland Railways.

New Zealand's first railway was a 914 mm (3 ft) gauge mining line at Nelson, opened in 1862. Strict supervision by the central government prevented a repetition of the Australian gauge problem. True, around Canterbury there were many miles of 1600 mm (5 ft 3 in) gauge track, but in 1870 a committee

reported on the gauge question, and recommended the 1067 mm (3 ft 6 in) gauge as an excellent compromise, and this gauge was thereupon standardized. This decision for many decades was criticized by the public, who blamed it for the rather slow speeds of New Zealand trains. However, it was the cheap construction, with its sharp curves and difficult grades, which was really responsible for this dissatisfaction.

Locomotives had at first been imported from Britain, but there was a growing body of opinion which felt that because the New Zealand track standards were closer to America than to Britain, American-style locomotives would be more suitable. In 1878 a batch of American engines were obtained from Rogers, and these gave good service. But despite their capabilities, further purchases of American locomotives were opposed by those who thought that the traditional ties with Britain should not be spurned. Ten years later the best solution to the problem appeared when two locomotives were built in New Zealand itself. Henceforth, the New Zealand Government Railways locomotives were designed in New Zealand, and largely built in New Zealand.

New Zealand was a pioneer in the use of the classic 4–6–2 and 4–8–2 wheel arrangements; the term Pacific used for the 4–6–2 type derives from the South Pacific destination of this first batch of 4–6–2s delivered by the American Baldwin works. Perhaps the most notable New Zealand locomotive type was the Ab class Pacific, which could haul 300-tonne passenger trains at over 80 km/h (50 mph) and 750-tonne freight trains at up to 48 km/h (30 mph). Later New Zealand locomotives in this mixed traffic

Left: An oil-burning Mallet-type locomotive working a branch passenger train in Java. Below: A New Zealand Railways Kb class 4–8–4 approaching Arthur's Pass with a freight train.

tradition were the K, Ka, and Kb class 4–8–4s built from the late 1930s. These were very powerful engines for the gauge, and could haul 500-tonne trains up 1 in 50 gradients. However, most of their work was in freight service.

By the early seventies regular steam operation had ceased in New Zealand and Australia, but further north, in the former Dutch East Indies, the Indonesian State Railways seemed likely to maintain steam services for a decade or two more; owing to lack of capital, diesel locomotives could only be bought for the most important services. The East Indian railways

Above: Three units of New South Wales's class 32
4–6–0 built by Beyer, Peacock, with an excursion train.

had their origin in 1867 when the Netherlands East
Indies Railway opened its first line from Semarang to
Tangoeng in Java. This line was standard gauge, but

in the west of Java a 1067 mm (3 ft 6 in) gauge line was
built to connect the capital Batavia (now Djakarta)
with the cool hill station at Bogor. Undeterred by the
gauge problems experienced by other colonial territories, the Dutch later permitted another undertaking,
the State Railway, to build further 1067 mm (3 ft 6 in)

gauge lines. By the turn of the century passengers by the southern route from Batavia to Surabaya started and finished their journey on the narrower gauge, but changed into a standard gauge train for the central section. The eventual laying of a third rail on the standard gauge section, so that the narrower gauge trains could operate the whole way, was some alleviation, but not a solution to the general Javanese gauge problem. On the other hand, in the 1930s the fastest train between Batavia and Surabaya held a world record for the fastest schedule on the 3 ft 6 in gauge.

While a majority of East Indian locomotives were of tank or tramway type, the heavy grades of some lines led to the import of some very large designs. Not only Mallet-type articulated locomotives were used, but also large tank locomotives of the unusual 2–12–2 wheel arrangement. After World War II the ageing locomotive stock was to some extent rejuvenated by the import from the German firm of Krupp of one hundred 2–8–2 mixed traffic locomotives. In the meantime the gauge problem had been solved by the Japanese invaders of 1942, who removed most of the standard gauge equipment to Manchuria, leaving the 3 ft 6 in gauge as the new standard gauge.

Since the 1960s, the steam locomotive has been ousted by diesels from the mainline passenger services, but it can still be found on secondary services. With its scant capital resources and the republic's enormous population Indonesian railways can hardly be expected to provide a European style of service. On the secondary lines trains run unreliably and irregularly, but that they run at all is a credit to those whose job it is to maintain, in face of a crucial shortage of spare parts, the usually antiquated steam locomotives and equally antiquated rolling stock.

Another Asian stronghold of the 3 ft 6 in gauge is Japan, which emerged from its self-imposed isolation just in time to benefit from the railway age. The new regime which took power in 1869 was committed to a programme of industrialization, militarization and westernization. Taking as its example that other and most successful island power, Great Britain, the new Japan based both its navy and its railways on the British model. With a loan floated on the London market, and despite the opposition of prophetic highway innkeepers and coolies, the first railway was opened in 1872. This 28 km (18 mile) line was from Tokyo to Yokohama, and to show that the venture had heavenly approval the Emperor himself was present at the inauguration. This was the beginning of the Japanese Imperial Railways. Two more important lines were soon opened by the government, from Osaka to Kyoto and Kobe. By 1877 the Japanese were able to plan the new Kyoto–Otsu line entirely with their own resources, although some of the actual construction was supervised by foreign engineers.

Like the Dutch railways, the Japanese railways had

Previous pages: A Mallet-type tank locomotive, built in Germany in 1909, is hand-turned on a manual turntable at the end of a branch line in Java.
Top: A 4–4–0, once a main line passenger engine, now working on a branch line in Java. Above: One of the 1951 batch of 2–8–2s supplied to Indonesia by Krupp.
Above right: A Japanese National Railways C62 class 4–6–4.
Right: One of the Japanese National Railways' more numerous classes was the class D52 2–8–2, a unit of which is shown about to take coal at a locomotive depot.

to struggle hard to obtain freight traffic, which because of Japan's geography was very suited to carriage by coastal shipping. Nevertheless, and partly because of the potential passenger traffic, private capital was eventually persuaded to invest in new lines. In fact there was a minor railway mania in the mid 1890s, with many unnecessary and hopelessly unprofitable lines being built. In the ensuing depression many of the private companies merged. As in Russia, the private lines tended to be more efficiently run, or at least more profitable, than the state lines, but for political reasons (and above all because the Japanese did not relish their transport arteries being under the control of mainly foreign capitalists) the most important companies were nationalized in the early 20th century. One of the arguments of the nationalizing lobby was that the new state railway administration would have the will and resources to replace the narrow gauge with the European standard gauge. Like the New Zealanders, the Japanese erroneously ascribed the shortcomings of their train service to the narrowness of their gauge.

Locomotives were at first imported, mainly from Britain but also from America and Germany. In time a domestic locomotive industry developed and a Japanese style of locomotive emerged. This tended to be of cleaner outline than the American locomotive, but less sleek than the European. In the last decades of steam traction the C62 class of 4–6–4, built in the late 1940s, was the most impressive of the Japanese designs, and was used on the main passenger services. For freight and secondary passenger service the 2–8–2 type was built; over a thousand units of the D51 class, followed by the improved D52, were built in the 1930s and 1940s. However, it was probably the C51 Pacific, which hauled fast passenger trains of traditional wooden-bodied vehicles in the inter-war years, which will be regarded as the archetypal Japanese locomotive.

Right: One of the Indian Railways standard broad gauge WG class 2–8–2 locomotives on a passenger working at Dinapur. These locomotives are used mainly for freight work, but are capable of hauling all but the fastest passenger trains.

Articulated locomotives

Like other engineers, steam locomotive designers had always to make compromises between conflicting possibilities and requirements. Managements asked for ever more powerful locomotives because heavier and faster trains not only reduced the costs of train crews, but also made it possible to handle growing traffic without the capital expense of new tracks or improved signalling. But the ability of a steam locomotive to exert greater power was limited by its adhesion to the track. Beyond a certain power output, and especially on rainy days, the driving wheels would begin to slip. Increasing the weight borne by the driving wheels was one way of improving this situation, but there were definite limits to this weight, the

Left: A Mallet locomotive of the Indonesian Railways, built in Switzerland in 1927, at work on a heavily graded branch line in Java. Below: Woodburning Beyer-Garratt locomotives used by the Benguela Railway in West Africa.

'axleload'. Rails would tend to break under high axle-loads and railway civil engineers were in an almost continuous state of conflict with mechanical engineers on this point. A measure dating from the very earliest locomotives was to couple the driving wheels with other wheels of the same diameter by means of coupling rods. The creation of extra driving wheels in this way spread the weight available for adhesion over several axles and thereby placed less stress on the rails. Although the *Rocket* had only a single pair of driving wheels, other Stephenson locomotives had two, and in the 1820s Timothy Hackworth of the Stockton and Darlington had built his *Royal George*, an 0–6–0 with three. After the 0–6–0 came the 2–6–0, 0–8–0 and 2–8–0 for freight work, and around the turn of the century the ten-coupled locomotive appeared, the 0–10–0, 2–10–0 and 2–10–2.

Although a few twelve-coupled locomotives were subsequently built, and even a 4–14–4 in Stalin's

Russia, ten-coupled wheels represented the limit for most railways, because with a long rigid wheelbase the wheels would grind against the rails on curves, leading at best to excessive wear and tear and at worst to derailment. It was evident therefore that if locomotives of greater power were still required, and they were, new solutions would have to be found. Such solutions took the form of the articulated locomotive, in which the driving wheels were divided into more than one set, with at least one of the sets being able to swivel.

Although it was not until the end of the 19th century that the articulated locomotive became significant, credit for the first such locomotive probably belongs to Horatio Allen, the enterprising engineer of America's South Carolina Railroad who in 1832 introduced three locomotives which consisted essentially of two 2–2–0 locomotives back to back, with a flexible joint between the two. However, these were not very successful. Four later designers, however, made a success of their own interpretation of the articulation concept. They were the Scotsman Robert Fairlie, the Alsatian J. Meyer, the Franco-Swiss Anatole Mallet, and the Englishman Herbert Garratt.

The locomotives of the first two were built mainly for narrow-gauge or branch lines, whereas it was Garratt and Mallet locomotives which would be regarded as the giants of the steam age.

Meyer patented his articulated locomotive in 1861 and the first example was built in 1868. It had a single boiler and two engine units, or power bogies, to which were attached the couplings and buffing gear. The cylinders were at the inner end of each unit, so they were all beneath the centre of the boiler. Later engines built in Germany were compounds, the used steam from one engine unit being used in the larger cylinders of the other. Many tank engines of this compound variety were built for narrow-gauge lines in Saxony (now in the German Democratic Republic) and some are still at work there.

What later became known as the Fairlie locomotive was patented in 1864. This was an articulated machine which its inventor intended for use on narrow-gauge railways, which required powerful locomotives for their twisting and heavily graded lines, which were usually of light rail. The first was built in 1865 for the Neath and Brecon Railway in south Wales. It had two pivoting power bogies and a pair of back-to-back

54

boilers. There was thus a chimney and smokebox at each end and a common firebox at the centre, the cab being built around this firebox. This type was known as the Fairlie 'double-ender' although the inventor did produce a single-boiler variety and Mason in the USA built a single-boiler variant for use on American narrow-gauge lines. Fairlie double-enders had their most spectacular success on the Festiniog Railway in Wales (one of the Festiniog units is illustrated on page 62). Observers from many parts of the world visited Festiniog to see the prodigious haulage capacity of the narrow-gauge machines. The Russian delegation was so impressed that narrow-gauge lines were started in Russia, and one broad-gauge line ordered a series of Fairlie double-enders for its line through the Caucasian mountains. However, the majority of Fairlie engines failed to make their expected mark. As with other articulated designs, the basic problem was how to design a flexible but tight steampipe joint so that steam could be passed to cylinders fixed to swivelling bogies. Fairlie devised a very effective joint (later copied by Garratt for his own locomotives) but such a joint required careful and frequent maintenance. This it frequently did not receive, so that steam which should have passed to the cylinders escaped into the atmosphere.

It was this steam joint problem which first aroused

Anatole Mallet's interest in the articulated locomotive. As engineer of the French Bayonne–Biarritz Railway, he had attracted engineering attention in 1877 by putting into service two two-cylinder locomotives using his own compound system. But although they worked quite well and certainly economically, he was unable to interest the mainline railways in compounding. Fervently believing in the rightness of the compounding cause, he seized upon the well-known defect of the Fairlie and Meyer engines. He proposed to build an articulated locomotive in which the rear power bogie would be rigidly fixed to the boiler, and the forward bogie pivoted beneath the chimney. The steam pipe to the rear cylinders would no longer need a flexible joint, while if the locomotive were a compound only the once-used (and hence low-pressure) steam from the rear cylinders would need to pass through a flexible joint to feed the forward cylinders. With low-pressure steam the problem of leakage at the joint would be largely solved.

Mallet was right in these forecasts. His early 0–4–4–0 tank locomotives built on these principles were used to convey passengers on a light railway laid to serve the 1889 Paris Exhibition. Their qualities thus received abundant publicity and many European short- or narrow-gauge lines ordered similar machines. More important, especially for American railroads, was the appearance of the Mallet tender locomotive, first ordered by Swiss and German railways in the 1890s. In 1904 the Baltimore and Ohio Railroad became the first American line to use a Mallet locomotive, the so-called 'two engines in one'. Unofficially

Left: A powerful 4–8–4 + 4–8–4 Beyer-Garratt locomotive of the East African Railways. Below: A small Mallet 2–6–6–2 locomotive built by Baldwin in the USA for a Brazilian line.

named *Old Maud*, the B and O unit was an 0–6–6–0 tender engine bought for pushing heavy trains up the Sand Patch incline. It was not long before further compound Mallets like *Old Maud* were built by US builders for other railroads, and henceforth the Mallet locomotive was a feature more of American railroads than European. One company which invested heavily in the type before World War 1 was the Santa Fe Railroad. Its enthusiasm led it to try to improve the type and it was probably the failure of these improvements which later drove it away from the concept, so that in the last decades of steam it was one of the few big US mountain lines which did not use the type. Among its earlier innovations were a pair of 4–4–6–2 Mallets for passenger work. But the pivoting of the forward power bogie was not really suitable for high-speed work, as the railroad soon discovered. The Santa Fe's next imaginative leap forward was a Mallet in which the boiler itself was flexible. It attempted to achieve this goal with a boiler made in two sections, joined by a concertina-like cylindrical joint. This was

one of those innovations which worked in theory and on trial, but was subsequently a constant source of trouble to those who had to work with it on a daily basis.

Another US development of the Mallet locomotive was the 'Triplex'. This had not two, but three power bogies, the third being located beneath the tender. The first was built for the Erie Railroad in 1914. It had 24 driving wheels, being a 2–8–8–8–2. Not many of this type were built, as the boiler could not supply the six cylinders with adequate steam; as their crews complained, these locomotives 'had too many legs'. Of the conventional Mallet types, the largest were the successful 2–10–10–2 units of the Virginian Railway, built by the American Locomotive Company in 1918.

These Virginian locomotives represented the peak of Mallet's original concept of a compound. Their low-pressure cylinders were 1219 mm (4 ft) in diameter, and even the generous American side clearances could hardly accommodate anything bigger. After 1918, therefore, there was an increasing demand

56

Above: Large low-pressure cylinders are evident in this pre-war colour picture of an American compound Mallet.

for the non-compound Mallet, which did not require large low-pressure cylinders. This was an abandonment of Mallet's original compound concept, but the anticipated troubles with the high-pressure flexible steam joint did not materialize, thanks to more modern manufacturing and maintenance techniques.

Unusual Mallet locomotives included those of the Southern Pacific Railroad, which had their cabs in front, so that smoke would be less of a nuisance in the tunnels through the Rockies. Then there were the *Alleghenies*, of which the Chesapeake and Ohio Railroad had 60 units; these had enormous 6-wheel trucks to support their capacious fireboxes, and were of the 2–6–6–6 wheel arrangement. For many years the Northern Pacific Railroad's 2–8–8–4 Mallets were regarded as the world's largest locomotives, but this record finally passed to the *Big Boys* of the Union Pacific. These 25 4–8–8–4 Mallets weighed 386

tonnes, could develop 7000 hp, and ran at 100 km/h (60 mph). They were a worthy successor to the same railroad's 110 *Challengers*. In the latter 4–6–6–4 type, the engineers of the railroad and of the builder succeeded in improving the pivoting of the leading power bogie so that these locomotives could run at higher speeds; in fact the *Challengers* sometimes hauled passenger trains, and could reach 130 km/h (80 mph) in safety.

At the peak of its popularity before World War 1 the Mallet locomotive was ordered by railways in several parts of the world, and some units were built under licence by European builders. In fact the last Mallets to survive in regular service were ordered for the Dutch East Indies and built in both America and Europe. But it was only in America that the type retained its market right up to the end of the steam era. The Garratt articulation system, developed later, was somewhat superior, especially before the Union Pacific Railroad had solved the Mallet's stability problems. But the American railroads evidently felt that the Mallet type was good enough, for they showed no interest in the Garratt idea, even though one American locomotive builder took the precaution of obtaining building rights for the type.

Herbert Garratt, after much experience with colonial-type railways, returned to England and patented his locomotive in 1907. At first he had some trouble in interesting the British locomotive builders in his idea, even though it seemed to solve some of the traction problems of British colonial railways. In his system there were two engine units, widely spaced, and the boiler was swung between them, with each of its ends pivoted on one of the units. The water tank was carried on one unit, while coal and an auxilliary tank were mounted on the other. This spread the weight of the locomotive, an important factor which made it possible to run heavy locomotives without the need to strengthen bridges and track. This load-spreading, and the flexible wheelbase obtained from the two pivots, was not the only advantage of the Garratt locomotive. The position of the boiler, literally in mid-air, solved one of the most common and largely unsolved problems of the locomotive designer, the question of how to mount a really adequate, deep, firebox with unimpeded air access.

It was the firm of Beyer Peacock, faced with a difficult requirement from a small Tasmanian railway, which first took up Garratt's idea and then built the subsequent engines of the type, which came to be described as Beyer–Garratts. Only when their order books were full were locomotives of this type manufactured under licence by other companies. After World War 1 the type became very popular both for narrow-gauge and mainline railways. In Britain itself only a few were ordered, some for hauling coal from the Midlands to London, and one unit for pusher service, but in the British Commonwealth they were very popular. In Africa the 1067 mm (3 ft 6 in) gauge South African Railways were early and enthusiastic customers, and the type was also successfully operated in the Rhodesias and East Africa. On the broad gauge, the Indian Bengal–Nagpur Railway began to operate 2–8–0+0–8–2 units on its coal trains. In fact, with the exception of North America, Garratts could be found on all continents. Admittedly, they were rare in Europe, but the Spanish railways had some notable passenger Garratts and in the early thirties even the Soviet Union ordered a unit for trial. The latter was the biggest Garratt ever built. It was a 4–8–2+2–8–4 which weighed 262 tonnes in working order but had an axle load of less than 20 tonnes. The order was not repeated, and although the Soviet engineers claimed

it was unsuitable for cold climates the real reason for the lack of further Russian orders was the Soviet shortage of foreign exchange. Another big Beyer–Garratt series was the batch of 4–8–4+4–8–4 units delivered to the New South Wales Railways in the 1950s. These weighed as much as the Russian unit, but because of the greater number of wheels, had an axleload of only 16 tonnes.

The drawback of the Garratt was, of course, the necessity for flexible steam joints. Because there were two pivots there were also two flexible joints, whereas the less supple Mallet had only one pivot and one joint. However, the extra maintenance requirement was not serious in colonial territories, where labour was cheap, and in other more developed parts of the world railway administrations evidently regarded the extra first cost and maintenance expenses as a small price to pay for a locomotive which could haul heavy loads at quite high speeds over lines that had been built relatively inexpensively.

Steam revived

Although the big American railroads eliminated steam traction in the 1950s and 1960s, and most of the European railways did so in the 1960s and 1970s, the steam locomotive in regular service seems likely to outlast the 20th century. In China steam locomotive construction is believed to be still continuing, and while in India steam locomotive construction ceased in 1972, new boilers have been built since then. These two nations have two features in common: they are developing countries in which rail traffic is growing rapidly so that even with electrification and dieselization they cannot afford to scrap steam locomotives, and they have plenty of coal. Elsewhere in the world South Africa and Indonesia have sizeable steam locomotive fleets. The steam locomotive would seem to be admirably suited to South Africa's current needs, for it burns local coal whereas diesels burn imported oil which is vulnerable to external political pressures. Despite this, South African railways have expressed the intention to dieselize at a rate which outside observers find puzzling. Nevertheless, even without a policy change steam traction seems likely to survive many more years in the republic. In Indonesia, while diesel traction has taken over the most important mainline passenger services, steam locomotives still handle the bulk of the secondary trains. Most of the latter are loss making, so the survival of the steam locomotive depends not so much on the fate of diesel imports (which Indonesia can hardly afford) but on the government's policy towards unprofitable lines. In most of Europe and in Australasia regular steam operation has disappeared. There are, however a few European countries making substantial use of steam locomotives. Prominent among these are Poland and East Germany, while Hungary entrusts many of its secondary passenger trains to modern 4–8–0s, and the Soviet Union still uses 0–10–0 and 2–10–0 locomotives on local freight work. In South America, too, steam lives on.

Above left: An 0–6–0 at work on the Bluebell Railway.
Left: Operable preserved steam locomotives from all over Britain assembled at Shildon in 1975 to celebrate 150 years of British railways.

The end of steam traction, accompanied as it was by much public regret at the passing of a familiar spectacle and a well-proven technology, brought an increased interest in railway museums, both static and working. As a result, in most countries where steam traction has ended many of the last classes of locomotive have been preserved. On the other hand, the number of preserved locomotives from earlier periods is rather small.

Preservation of the earlier locomotives was very much a matter of luck. Here and there a local museum of technology might save a well-known locomotive, or, more likely, a part or two from a locomotive. Sometimes the mechanical engineering department of a railway was reluctant to scrap the last member of a famous class, or a locomotive which had once broken records. Thus the Great Western Railway preserved at its Swindon works one of its first engines, *North Star*, and one of its best-loved broad-gauge single-driver locomotives. But these were sent for scrap early in this century by the chief mechanical engineer, whose enthusiasm for things new was accompanied by a lack of enthusiasm for things old. The great Western later tried to make amends for this by building a replica of *North Star*, incorporating parts of the original, but apart from oddments like a horsehair-stuffed buffer, retrieved from private use as a stool, little of the original locomotive had survived the scrapheap. Other relics preserved in railway workshops were luckier. Among the many old locomotives to survive in Britain were one of Edward Bury's early bar-framed engines from the Furness Railway, the high-wheeled *Cornwall* of the London & North Western, an old 0–6–0 of the North Eastern Railway, and several others. Moreover, because some of the very earliest locomotives worked many decades, surviving into an age which was prepared to regard them as important relics, several are preserved. Among them are Hedley's *Puffing Billy* and *Wylam Dilly*. Hackworth's early 0–6–0 *Samson*, exported to Nova Scotia in 1838, is now preserved there. Major parts of Robert Stephenson's *Rocket* have also survived and his similar *Invicta* is preserved near the

railway on which it worked, the Canterbury and Whitstable. Another Stephenson machine, *John Bull*, exported in 1831 to the Camden and Amboy Railroad, is preserved in the USA.

John Bull was presented to the National Museum in Washington by the Pennsylvania Railway. Another American railroad which did much for locomotive preservation was the Baltimore and Ohio, whose long-established locomotive museum still exists. Among several early American locomotives now preserved are the *De Witt Clinton* of 1831, Baldwin's *Pioneer*, and William Norris's *Lafayette*. Later 19th century locomotives preserved in the USA include the record-breaking 4–4–0 No 999, Baldwin's 0–8–0 *Memnon*, and a *Gowan & Marx*-type 4–4–0. Apart from the Baltimore and Ohio Railroad's collection, the National Museum in Washington, the Greenfield Museum near Detroit, and the Franklin Institute in Philadelphia have notable exhibits.

In England the York Railway Museum, supported by the London and North Eastern Railway, helped to save several famous locomotives at a time when their historic value was unappreciated by the general public. Among them were the Great Western's 4–4–0 *City of Truro*, the Great Northern's 4–4–2 *Henry Oakley*, and the London, Brighton and South Coast Railway's 0–4–2 *Gladstone*, the latter being an early example of a locomotive rescued from the scrapheap by railway enthusiasts (in this case the Stephenson Locomotive Society). Soon after the railways were nationalized it was decided to centralize the York and other collections at a new transport museum in Clapham, London. But before this was fully achieved another decision established a new museum at York, in a former locomotive depot. When this new York National Railway Museum opened in 1975 it could claim to be the world's finest. Above all, unlike other national museums, it had the space properly to display its exhibits. Several of its locomotives are in working condition, and are periodically allowed to haul excursion trains.

Another new national railway museum with the advantage of spaciousness is that of Indian Railways at Delhi. The new French Museum at Mulhouse and the older-established display at Utrecht in Holland also have the space they need. (Early passenger rolling stock in these French and Dutch museums is shown on page 11). On the other hand, several national museums, including that of the German railways at Nurnberg, of the Hungarian at Budapest, the Romanian at Bucharest, the Austrian at Vienna and the Belgian at Brussels, have at present space to exhibit only one or two of their locomotive exhibits. However, they take very seriously their educative function, supplementing their display of relics with models and diagrams. Sectioned locomotives, with one half cleanly cut away to show the interior arrange-

Left: A Fairlie-type locomotive hauling a train of tourists on the Festiniog Railway in Wales. Top: The last steam engine built for British railways, the 2–10–0 'Evening Star', based at the York National Railway museum, still appears on excursions. Above: Two more exhibits from the National Railway Museum at York which have appeared on excursion work—the London and North Western 2–4–0 'Hardwicke' and the Midland compound 4–4–0 No 1000.

ment, are a feature of several museums, the Swiss Transport Museum at Lucerne being a pioneer in this form of display.

In the last years of steam the national railway museums were supplemented by collections of loco-motives acquired by individuals or railway societies. In Britain these include the collections of locomotives at Tyseley, Carnforth, and Bressingham, among others. In Australia the various state enthusiast organizations have invested much time and money in building up valuable and well-displayed collections. Some of their exhibits are operable and make occasional excursions. In North America the large number of privately-owned collections make it hard to pick out just a few for mention; two of the biggest are Steamtown in Vermont, and the Montreal railway museum.

Static exhibitions of locomotives, however instructive, do not convey the steam railway scene as a whole. The appearance, still less the sound and indeed the smell, of a steam locomotive at work can only be reproduced by running 'live steam'. In countries where regular steam operation has ceased this has been achieved in two ways: by running steam-hauled excursions over mainline railway track, and by reviving lines closed by the mainline railways and operating them as tourist attractions with steam motive power. In both these enterprises it has usually, although not

always, been railway enthusiast organizations which have taken the lead, supplied the labour, and found the capital.

The running of steam-hauled excursions originated long before the end of steam. As early as 1938 a British enthusiasts' society persuaded the London and North Eastern Railway to run a special train hauled by a preserved 4–2–2 locomotive, Great Northern No 1. In North America there were similar excursions using obsolete or historic locomotives. In Canada, the 'Foliage Excursion' became an annual event, with enthusiasts organizing autumn trips behind obsolete locomotives to view the brilliant colours of the northern woodlands. In this way was achieved what was so important for this kind of activity, a successful combination of what the enthusiast wanted to do with what the general public would be prepared to pay for.

As the age of steam drew to a close, British Railways took several preserved locomotives back into service to haul excursion trains. Among these were Caledonian Railway No 123 and the Great Western *City of Truro*. In Australia the state railway administrations, sometimes with the assistance of enthusiast organizations, assembled 'vintage trains' from old locomotives and rolling stock. These offered excursions and also served as the railways' exhibits at local centenary or other celebrations. In North America, as well as else-

Left: Most Dutch steam activity involves small tank locomotives on very short lines, but the 4–6–0 No 3737 was temporarily released from the Utrecht museum to haul weekend excursions. Right: Another view of British steam locomotives assembling for a grand 'steam-past' at the 1975 celebrations at Shildon. The nearest locomotive is a 'Jubilee' class 4–6–0 of the London Midland and Scottish Railway, built in the 1930s.

where, the closing of a line or the withdrawal of a well-known locomotive type were typical occasions marked by a steam-hauled excursion.

The steam-hauled excursion has flourished, though not consistently, since the end of steam traction in America and western Europe. Locomotives reprieved from the scrapheap and, typically, restored to operating condition by voluntary and painstaking labour, have been used. In Britain, celebrated locomotives like *King George V, Flying Scotsman*, or one of the preserved streamlined Pacifics of Sir Nigel Gresley have perhaps hauled more than their fair share of such trains, but many other locomotives have participated. In this activity the attitude of the mainline railways is crucial. In Britain this has varied from frank non-cooperation to the present situation where organizations are allowed to run a limited number of excursions on a limited number of routes. In the USA the existence of many railway companies, some enthusiastic, some uninterested, and some hostile, has meant that it has always been possible, somewhere, to run an excursion; the main problem, usually solved, has been to attract enough passengers willing to pay a sufficiently high price to recompense the organizers. The running of steam trains, and especially maintaining a steam locomotive in working order, is very expensive. In the USA, too, a select few of the many preserved

and operable locomotives seem to draw the majority of excursions. In recent years these have included the Union Pacific 4–8–4 No 8444, of a class regarded by many as the final flowering of the American passenger locomotive, the Reading Railroad's 4–8–4 No 2102 and the Nickel Plate Railroad's 2–8–4 No 759. For the celebrations of the US Bicentenary a 'Freedom Train' was exhibited throughout the country and to haul it one of the Southern Pacific's celebrated 4–8–4s was brought out of retirement.

In Canada the Canadian National Railways, perhaps conscious of the publicity value of perpetuating memories of Canada's railway heritage, has been a frequent scene of steam excursions. For several years it made available 4–8–4 No 6218, a representative of a class which was once the main element of its motive power. When No 6218 became due for an expensive overhaul, the CNR decided it would be cheaper, and more interesting, to substitute another locomotive. So No 6079, a more modern 4–8–2, was taken down from its plinth and restored to service. In France, after a flurry of steam excursions to mark the end of steam traction, there have been occasional ventures, but organizers are deterred by the scarcity of operable mainline locomotives. At present a 4–6–0, No 230G-353 serves both for excursions and for film-making (its last film was *Orient Express*), but this locomotive

Above: 4–8–4 No 8444 with an excursion in Wyoming. Formerly No 844, this locomotive was one of a class built to haul the Union Pacific Railroad's transcontinental passenger trains.

is hardly representative of the great age of French steam. In West Germany, where steam traction only ended in 1977, the prospects are clouded. Although German Railways organized several end-of-steam excursions in 1976–77, and although there are several operable locomotives available, it is doubtful whether frequent steam excursions will be permitted. However, the German railway enthusiast will not be entirely deprived of his favourite spectacle, because already several German steam locomotives have operated excursions over the neighbouring tracks of the Netherlands Railways.

The reopening with steam traction of lines previously closed became commonplace in Europe and America in the 1960s and 1970s. An influential pioneer among railway preservation societies was that of the Talyllyn Railway of 1950, which restored this moribund Welsh slate-carrying line to a passenger-carrying tourist attraction. Using the existing rolling stock, later supplemented by appropriate locomotives and passenger vehicles from other narrow-gauge lines, the volunteers of this society created a flourishing railway enterprise whose commercial success encouraged the creation of other tourist railways. An early standard-gauge line was the Bluebell Railway, which took over a length of abandoned railway in Sussex and refurbished it with an interesting collection of vintage rolling stock. Running passenger trains at weekends and during the summer holidays, it too attracted a wide public and thereby attained commercial success. Meanwhile, in Wales several other narrow-gauge lines were transformed. Most interesting of these was the old Festiniog Railway. It was not long before the restored Welsh narrow-gauge lines, with the unchanged Vale of Rheidol narrow-gauge line still owned by British Rail, coordinated their public relations

under the name of 'The Great Little Trains of Wales'. With moral and financial support from the Welsh Tourist Board, and location in a popular tourist area, their future seemed assured so long as they could attract the voluntary unpaid labour of railway enthusiasts to supplement their small regular staffs.

Elsewhere in Britain other steam railways have been created on the pattern of the Bluebell line. Some are commercial, and others purely amateur. Several are the result of a sometimes uneasy partnership between commercial interests and devoted enthusiasts. Among the more notable lines are the Torbay Steam Railway

Left: A steam excursion in France: 4-6-0 No 230G-353 at Beauvais, on the former Nord Railway, hauling a train of vintage Nord Railway rolling stock. Below left: At the Henry Ford Museum at Greenfield Village, a 4-4-0 is the centrepiece of a representation of a 19th century railway scene. Right: Inside a vintage American day coach, with traditional centre aisle and reversible seats. This example runs on the Cass Scenic Railroad in West Virginia. Below: The narrow gauge Silverton train in Colorado, hauled by 2-8-2 No 478, complete with spark arrestor chimney.

in Devon, which recreates the atmosphere of a Great Western branch line, the Keighley and Worth Valley, situated in a scenic and historic part of Yorkshire, and the Severn Valley Railway, passing through pleasant scenery and close enough to Birmingham to attract a useful number of day-trippers.

In Australia there is the so-called 'Puffing Billy Line', a narrow-gauge enterprise in the Dandenong Range near Melbourne. In New South Wales a section of abandoned main line is available for excursions by museum locomotives. In New Zealand the state railway has itself established the 'Kingston Flyer' tourist line, operating in the summer, and has set aside a pair of Pacific locomotives to haul it.

Short tourist lines are also flourishing in continental Europe. One of the first, and most successful, has been the Vivarais line in France. Again, this is a line which has the advantage of beautiful scenery already well-known to tourists. It is a former metre-gauge local railway and uses Mallet-type tank locomotives of the type which once worked freight traffic on the line. In Holland, Germany, Switzerland, Sweden, Denmark, Belgium and Hungary there are also active steam short lines, usually operating at selected weekends. In

Austria there are several steam narrow-gauge lines operated by their original owners and dividing their activities between tourists and their regular traffic.

In America, the 1950s and 1960s were the great years for the opening of steam short lines. By 1968 there were almost 50 such lines distributed around the USA, with a preponderance in the north eastern states and in California. Among the early lines were the Strasburg Railroad, situated in the tourist 'Dutch Country' area of Pennsylvania, and the East Broad Top, a former coal line in Pennsylvania. The East Broad Top succeeded admirably in using old equipment to recreate a real vintage atmosphere, but suffered commercially because it was not situated in a tourist area.

One of the most ambitious and most successful ventures was the Silverton Train. This runs in the summer over a long stretch of the narrow-gauge trackage formerly operated by the Rio Grande Railroad in Colorado. It provides the longest ride (144 km or 90 miles) of all the US lines, using three 2–8–2

locomotives which the Rio Grande bought for narrow-gauge freight service in 1923. Because of the tourist attractions of the Colorado mountains, and skilful publicity (helped, as is often the case, by the state's own publicity service), the line was attracting 80,000 passengers annually by the mid 1960s. This was by no means the highest passenger total; much shorter lines, situated in the right areas, measure their customers in not tens of thousands but in hundreds of thousands. One commercial line, that of Disneyland, carries millions annually, but few railway enthusiasts would concede that this line really belongs to the vintage railway movement.

Indeed, in Britain as well as America, there have been occasional conflicts between the strict railway historical interest, and the commercial interest. The problem, which each line has to solve in its own way, is that in order to keep steam engines running for the benefit of present and future generations money has to be earned from the general public. That public is less interested in preserving the short lines strictly as

Far left: A 4–6–2 and 2–8–0 on a steam excursion near Atlanta. Above: Nickel Plate 2–8–4 No 759 in excursion service. Left: The Canadian National's 4–8–4 No 6218 hauling a steam excursion in Ontario.

they were than in having an exciting day out. Some lines have therefore indulged in staging attractions, varying from mock Indian raids on some US short lines to fancy paint schemes which bear no resemblance to the colours worn by locomotives and cars in the old days. Most of the lines have managed to reach acceptable compromises, but there have been sporadic acrimonious outbursts from enthusiasts who, having given up their spare time to accurately restore a railway, have found the more commercial railway management introducing eye-catching anachronisms. But the threatening truth remains that unless the tourist lines can accumulate adequate capital, they will not be able to run their steam locomotives when major components such as boilers require replacement or extensive repair. In theory, a steam locomotive is immortal, for each part as it wears out can be replaced; many old locomotives were kept in service so long that hardly an original part remained. But nowadays, because of the cessation of steam locomotive building, components are much more expensive.

Top: Several batches of British Railways' earlier diesel locomotives employed the German hydraulic transmission. Here is one of them, of the 'Warship' class, approaching Reading. Above: The New York to Florida route still generates a profitable passenger traffic and trains like this, operated by the Seaboard Coast Line when photographed, have been continued under Amtrak auspices. Right: Two twin-car units of a post-war French railcar design passing through Picardy.

Passenger trains after steam

The most obvious change in passenger train operation over recent decades has been the replacement of steam by electric and diesel traction. It was in the USA that the shape of things to come was first seen. There, the internal combustion engine was in use on the railways before World War 1, powering the 'gas-electric' railcar. These railcars, with their gasoline engines driving a generator which in turn powered electric traction motors, were a partial solution to the branch line problem, where passenger services had to be provided for a clientele too small to justify a locomotive-hauled train. However, the gasoline engine was not really suited for railway use and was soon superseded by the diesel which, too, was first applied to railway use in the early years of this century. In 1912 the Swedish State Railway put into service a passenger railcar having a diesel engine with electric transmission, and this proved very satisfactory.

However, the acceptance by the railways of diesel traction came very slowly. Partly this was due to the conservatism of railway managements, whose instinctive traditionalism was boosted by the continual improvement in steam locomotive performance and the problems of designing a really outstanding diesel locomotive. The diesel locomotive designer's problem was the difficulty of converting the high-speed revolutions of the diesel engine to the slow revolutions of the locomotive wheel. Technically the easiest method was to drive a generator from the fast-rotating diesel shaft, and then feed the electricity so produced to electric traction motors driving the wheels. Such traction motors were simple and had long been in use on electric tramways and electric railways. But generators were heavy and expensive, two factors which greatly reduced the diesel locomotive's theoretical advantage in power per tonne of locomotive, and made the first cost of a diesel locomotive about three times greater than that of a corresponding steam locomotive.

In the inter-war years great efforts were made to develop a non-electric transmission, and many railway administrations postponed buying diesels until such a transmission, believed imminent, appeared. However it was not until the eve of World War II that a promising hydraulic transmission was developed in Germany. For a time, in the 1950s and 1960s, it seemed that this might indeed replace the electric transmission, but in recent years improvements in the latter have resulted in its continued predominance.

Below: The Canadian National Railways' 'Super Continental' leaving Montreal for Vancouver in 1957.

Previous pages: A line-up of Netherlands Railways rolling stock of the early 1960s. Left: A modern diesel-electric passenger locomotive used by Amtrak for its fastest locomotive-hauled trains. Below left: The 'Southerner', one of the best trains of New Zealand Railways, which covers the 594 km (369 miles) from Christchurch to Invercargill in ten hours. Below: The economy class bar of the 'Indian Pacific', considered essential by Australians making the 66-hour, 3961 km (2460 mile) journey from Sydney to Perth. Right: The 'Indian Pacific' hauled by a Western Australian Railways diesel-electric locomotive. Because of the flat terrain, fewer locomotive units are required than would be the case in America.

The inter-war development of the diesel locomotive followed two paths. There were efforts, starting in Russia and Germany, to build a workable freight diesel locomotive. These were not entirely satisfactory, but in the late 1930s General Motors in the USA demonstrated its first diesel-electric freight locomotive, which was so successful that it virtually assured the eventual triumph of diesel traction. Simultaneously, several countries were experimenting with the high-speed diesel-powered train. Again, it was in the USA that the most spectacular progress was made, for in 1934 there appeared the railroads' answer to the automobile and the airliner. The Union Pacific and the Burlington railroads introduced, almost simultaneously, two different streamlined trains, powered by internal combustion.

Probably the intense publicity campaign which preceded and accompanied the appearance of these two trains was unnecessary, for they would have captured the headlines in any case. They incorporated many of the external elements of the new age, notably highly-fashionable streamlining. Both were three-car units. The Union Pacific's *M-10000* had a distillate

engine and the Burlington's *Zephyr* a true diesel. The Union Pacific's M-10001, which soon followed, was a 6-car unit with a diesel. All used electric transmission. The *Zephyr* was first into service, between Lincoln and Kansas City. However M-10001, named *City of Portland*, became the first of the transcontinental streamliners, reducing the Chicago–Portland schedule by 21 hours to just under 40 hours. Many a US railroad, discovering that its patrons were now demanding that they too should be provided with modern streamlined trains, simply refurbished existing rolling stock, cloaked a handful of steam locomotives in smooth sheet metal, and presented the resulting creation as its latest streamliner. The Chicago and North Western's *400* train from Chicago to St Paul was one such train, and it received as much praise from the local press as did the new diesel streamliners of other railroads. However, it was one of the latter, the Gulf, Mobile, and Northern's *Rebel* between Chicago and Kansas City, that was the real forerunner of the future American passenger train, for it was not a self-propelled train set, but a train of freely detachable cars hauled by a diesel locomotive.

The fast schedules which the new diesel stream-liners made possible were due less to high speed than to the ability to run long distances without the need to stop for water (track troughs, permitting steam loco-motives to take water without stopping, were rare in America). When on a demonstration run in connec-tion with the Chicago Exhibition the *Zephyr* averaged 120 km/h (77 mph) it could be argued that the steam locomotive was also capable of such speeds. But the *Zephyr*'s run had been of 1640 km (1015 miles), and no steam locomotive could equal that non-stop performance.

Such were the pressures of international publicity that in other countries the American example was soon followed by several railways. Many, like the two larger British companies, the French, Belgians, Germans and Japanese, produced some very capable streamlined steam locomotives, while making weak attempts to argue that streamlining brought significant fuel economy. But internal-combustion power was exploited by some managements; the French and Germans, in particular, developed the railcar. In France the high-speed railcar, sometimes streamlined like a Bugatti racing car, attracted much attention, but the main achievement of the French was in developing a varied range of railcars for secondary services. By 1938, when French railways were nationalized, no fewer than one quarter of the passenger train miles were contributed by a fleet of 650 such railcars.

Germany, the birthplace of the late Dr Rudolf Diesel, was naturally another country in which rail-

way diesel traction received much attention. In the pre-war years this was most evident in the railcar field. So important a place in secondary services was won by diesel railcars that during World War II oil short-ages compelled a substantial reduction in passenger services. However, in the 1930s it was the high-speed diesel train which won the limelight. The *Flying Hamburger* was a high-powered twin-car unit which, introduced on the Hamburg–Berlin run in 1933, averaged 125 km/h (78 mph) over the 287 km (179 miles). At about the same period, the Danish Railways introduced their *Lyntog* trains, which were high-speed diesel multiple units linking the main cities. In Britain the streamlined steam locomotive was still preferred to the high-speed diesel, but the Great Western Railway did successfully introduce 38 diesel railcars for use on lightly-loaded services.

The period after World War II brought a crisis for the passenger train in most of the more affluent countries. This happened first in the USA, where both the internal airline and the private car multiplied more rapidly than elsewhere. The peak year for passenger numbers in the USA had been 1916, although in terms of passenger-miles another wartime year, 1944, had been the peak. After 1944 American passenger traffic began its dramatic decline. The American railroads reacted by withdrawing as many of their unprofitable services as the state and federal governments would allow (the Interstate Commerce Commission, as well as individual state governments could compel railroads to maintain services, and often

Right: One of the oldest and best-known of the few British Pullman trains, the electric 'Brighton Belle' in 1962.
Far right: Austrian railways still carry a heavy passenger traffic, much of it international. However, the modern electric multiple unit at the right of this picture was designed for fast internal services. Below: Urban rail transport takes a variety of forms such as tramways, conventional railways and underground railways. The monorail, regarded as a cheap alternative to the underground and almost equally economical in land use, remains rare. This is the oldest of the more successful monorails, at Wuppertal in Germany, and dates from 1901.

did). At the same time, to retain the more profitable long-distance passengers, new and more alluring trains were introduced. In place of the traditional heavy, drably-painted passenger car, with its back-breaking day-coach seats and its open, unsecluded sleeping berths, there entered into service new light-weight alloy rolling stock, finished in stainless steel or painted to match the brightly coloured diesel locomotives. The small but cunningly designed roomette enabled passengers, for a slight increase of price over the traditional open berth, to enjoy the complete privacy previously obtainable only by the passenger affluent enough to afford a bedroom. In the day-coaches reclining seats were provided, of airline style but much more roomy than airline seating. To emphasize the sightseeing potentiality of the passenger train, the dome car was introduced. This had a glass-topped upper deck from which passengers could get a good view of the scenery.

Despite these innovations, patronage continued to decline. Since the railroads' freight operations were also under pressure, many companies faced bank-ruptcy, and it was said that the best way to help them would be to relieve them of the requirement of provid-ing passenger services. Since the total withdrawal of

passenger services was politically unacceptable, in 1971 a quasi-governmental agency, Amtrak, was established to take over the passenger trains of all railroads which wished to participate in the scheme. Most, but not all, railroads joined. Their task, in return for shedding the financial burden of their passenger services, was to hand over their passenger equipment to Amtrak and to work Amtrak trains over their lines as required. Insofar as the passenger train still operates in America, the scheme has been successful, but Amtrak's future is not yet assured. It still does not make a profit; it lost credit during the 1976–77 winter by its temporary withdrawal of services, and it had the misfortune of ordering a large batch of passenger diesel locomotives which proved unstable at high speeds. And despite Amtrak, the number of passenger services remains very small compared with the 1950s. In 1956, for example, five different railroads offered nineteen daily services from New York to Chicago, and several of these were all-sleeper trains. Twenty years later Amtrak offered one combined sleeper and day-coach train over the former New York Central route and one over the Pennsylvania's route (by which time both railroads, having unsuccessfully merged into the Penn-Central, were

absorbed in another quasi-governmental organization, Conrail, devised to preserve these and other unprofitable eastern railroads). On the other hand, Amtrak's fast electric *Metroliner* multiple-units in the densely trafficked north-east corridor route between New York and Washington have won back passengers from the private car and the airlines.

The *Metroliners* have been worthy successors of the frequent, fast, electrically-hauled trains which the Pennsylvania Railroad once provided between New York and Washington—well-known trains like *The Congressional* and *The Senator*. Very few of the famous train names have survived into the Amtrak era. The New York Central's celebrated *Empire State Express* and *Twentieth Century Limited* have disappeared from the timetable, while their one-time rival, the Pennsylvania's *Broadway Limited*, is no longer an all-sleeper train. What were reputed as the most luxurious of the transcontinental trains, the Santa Fe's *El Capitan* and *Super Chief*, were transferred to Amtrak but the Santa Fe soon stipulated that their names should no longer be used, as it doubted whether Amtrak would maintain the standard of service which the names promised. However, the *Empire Builder* transcontinental of the Great Northern, still runs, under Amtrak colours.

To a large degree, the best examples of the American-style long distance train now operate in Canada and Australia. However, the Canadian Pacific's *Canadian* and the Canadian National's *Super Continental*, unable to make a profit, are being replaced by a single train, timed to enable passengers to sleep not on board, but in accommodation at the nights' stopping places. This idea has already materialized with Amtrak's *Sunset Limited*, which runs from New York to California via New Orleans; in this case, however, the passenger has a day's sightseeing in New Orleans, using his sleeping compartment as a hotel. Australia is probably where the most luxurious all-sleeper train operates. This is the *Indian Pacific*, introduced after the completion of the standard gauge coast-to-coast link to provide a through service between Perth and Sydney. The first-class-only *Southern Aurora* night service between Melbourne and Sydney also has the kind of reputation enjoyed by the best American trains of two decades ago.

In Europe, with its shorter distances, internal airline competition has been less serious. But airlines' 'package' holidays have meant the diversion from the railways of the bulk of the summer traffic to southern Europe. On the other hand, the Trans European Express (TEE) trains, first introduced in the 1950s, have been fairly successful in countering the airlines' threat to first-class passenger traffic. The TEE is a de-luxe high-speed service aimed primarily at the businessman, who does not resent the supplementary fare which is levied. Apart from its comfort, high running speed, and thoughtfully timed departures, the TEE offers simplified customs procedures on board the train, various on-train services, good catering, and train hostesses. (Although the hostess, like reclining seats and other refinements, was in imitation of the airlines, it is noteworthy that she was not entirely new; the American *Rebel* of 1935 appears to have been the first train to have offered this attraction.)

The French and the German railways, in particular, still derive much revenue from the long-distance second-class passenger. That economic form of

sleeper travel, the couchette, enables six passengers to be fitted into one compartment and thereby permits fairly small extra charges to be levied for this facility. For many passengers travelling between 300 and 1000 miles (480 and 1600km) an overnight sleeper from city centre to city centre, apart from being less expensive, is as convenient as an airliner. The earliest TEE trains were diesel powered train sets, designed by the participating railways. But on many routes their success led to the substitution of more capacious locomotive-hauled trains. By 1977, for example, there

Top left: One of the modern generation of high-speed German electric locomotives. Left: Two interior views of the French 'Mistral'. Above: The 'Mistral' about to leave Marseilles.

were six TEE services in each direction between Paris and Brussels, each consisting of from six to ten cars, offering up to 350 seats, with meals served at each seat by staff of the International Sleeping Car Company. The TEE standard soon won a high reputation, and a few trains of the same designation were introduced by individual railways for internal services. Two services from Paris to Bordeaux, using de-luxe rolling stock with separate dining car, are among the more successful of these.

In Britain the advent of diesel traction was reflected in a gradual improvement of schedules, although on the East Coast route from London to Scotland and Newcastle there was a radical acceleration when a class of twenty 3000hp *Deltic* diesel-electric locomotives were introduced. Pullman trains, featuring more comfortable seating and meal service at all seats, had a limited application for some years but were then reduced to just four services. This reduction of Pullman service entailed the withdrawal of some celebrated long-lived trains, including the *Golden Arrow* from London to Paris and the *Brighton Belle*

service to the south coast. The more spectacular improvements in train service came only with electrification and, later, with the HST diesel trains. In the meantime, passenger deficits were reduced by the closing of branch lines and withdrawal of secondary services, measures which to some extent were paralleled on the railways of other developed countries. As elsewhere, too, the diesel railcar set or even the single unit railbus replaced the more expensive locomotive-hauled train on the remaining secondary services. An early innovation in Britain was the 'Inter City' appellation, which applied the 'brand-image' concept to a select group of passenger routes offering a service which could be described as superior in speed, comfort, and frequency. Britain's first air-conditioned cars were introduced on some of these services in the 1970s (air-conditioning, however, had been introduced years earlier on American railways and in a few hot countries).

To recapture the private car owner, railways also developed the car-sleeper train, in which the passengers' own cars were loaded on to flatcars which were attached to a train of sleeping cars in which the drivers and their passengers travelled. Aimed mainly at holiday traffic, such trains enjoyed great popularity in the summer north-to-south services of the continental railways. They were also used on such British routes

as from Scotland to the West of England. In the USA a private company provided the same service, rather more lavishly, between Washington and Florida. This company, *Auto-Train*, was independent of both Amtrak and the railroads; it merely paid the latter to haul its trains between terminals and railroadmen were not allowed inside the trains.

Because there were few lines with a sufficiently intensive traffic to make it worthwhile, only a few American main lines were electrified. At present only the trains of the north-east corridor and the longer-distance trains to the south which use the electrified tracks as far as Washington are electric. In Europe, however, the electric train has long been important. First introduced on short suburban lines before World War I, usually using low voltage current

Above left: Modern French passenger rolling stock.
Below left: A French electric locomotive on a test pad.
Above: A doubledeck suburban train of the Chicago
and North Western Railroad.

supplied through a third rail, most European railways
by World War II had long stretches of line electrified
with overhead catenary. An exception was Britain,
where electrification was confined to lines in southern
England, and these used third rail in conformity with
the suburban lines of which they were extensions. By
1939 Italy had the greatest electrified mileage but
some countries, notably Switzerland, were approaching complete electrification. Because it was so reliable,
because it permitted the use of high-horsepower
locomotives, and because it was suited to a high-
frequency service, electrification did much to retain
passengers for the railways. The destruction of World
War II with its consequent writing-off of much steam-
age infrastructure, meant that electrification in many
countries (again with the exception of Britain) was
accelerated. In France, where lines from Paris to
Bordeaux and Toulouse had long been electrified, the
conversion of the heavy-traffic Paris–Marseilles line
was undertaken. After this was finished, the electric
Mistral, running from Paris to the Mediterranean,
became not only a record-breaker but a symbol to all
the world that the fast, convenient and comfortable
passenger train was far from dead. Trains like this
enhanced the reputation of French engineers (who
began to receive electrification contracts from other
countries), encouraged proponents of the passenger
train in other countries, and aroused a demand from
the public for trains as good as the French trains.
Subsequent French services, like the new fast trains

averaging over 128 km/h (80 mph) in the Paris–Lille
service, and the *Aquitaine* from Paris to Bordeaux,
enhanced this reputation, even though Japan and
perhaps Britain have now overtaken France as operators of high-speed trains.

In Britain the electrification of the old London and
North Western main line from London to Birmingham, Manchester and Liverpool was an opportunity,
fully taken, to introduce a completely new service of
frequent, comfortable, and fast trains. The enterprise
soon brought satisfying commercial results for not
only was the decline of traffic halted but new traffic
was created, while many motorists decided that the
train was, after all, better. The same dramatic improvement was not forthcoming when this electrification was extended to Scotland, but nevertheless the
competitive position of the railway (in this case in
relation to the airline), was plainly strengthened.
Electric traction was especially effective in cutting
schedules over the heavily graded section between
Carnforth and Carlisle. The 50 km (31 miles) climb
to Shap Summit was covered by electric traction at an
average speed of 135 km/h (85 mph) compared with
the 86 km/h (54 mph) of the pre-war streamlined
Coronation Scot.

Even 128 km/h (80 mph) schedules were not considered by Japanese National Railways to be sufficient
to beat the competition. The fast train was to be
superseded by the high-speed train. A major step in
this direction was the construction of the New
Tokaido Line. This, the first stage of a proposed new
and supplementary network, was built to the 1435 mm
(4 ft 8½ in) standard gauge; it was claimed, probably
wrongly, that this was required for the high speeds

which were envisaged. But despite the disadvantage of creating a second gauge, the New Tokaido Line seemed to justify itself. The first section was opened in 1964 between Tokyo and Osaka. It was double-track, engineered to very high standards, and intended for passenger trains only (freight continued to use the existing narrower gauge line). Its electric 'bullet trains' reached speeds of up to 210 km/h (130 mph) and attracted many thousands of new passengers who seemed quite willing to pay the extra fare which was charged. The fares were only marginally below the corresponding air fares, so the initial transfer of passengers from air to rail was probably induced by service rather than financial considerations. But, like British Rail, Japanese National Railways found that when further lengths were opened, airline competition was harder to beat. As elsewhere, the 300–600 km (200–400 mile) journey was evidently the most promising field for railway passenger service.

The New Tokaido Line had the same beneficial effect on Japanese railway exports as had the French electrifications of the 1950s. However, the more developed railways began to introduce their own, rather than Japanese, concepts of the high speed train. The electric *Metroliners* ordered by the Penn-Central but operated by Amtrak between New York and Washington could be considered a first generation of such trains, even though the intended maximum speed of 255 km/h (160 mph) was not attainable in practice. A new departure was the gas turbine train

sets introduced by French National Railways in 1970 to provide fast services on important but unelectrified lines. The initial trains, which had a diesel engine at one end and a gas turbine at the other, were used to provide a fast and frequent service on the Paris–Cherbourg line. In 1977 these trains covered the 371 km /230 miles) in about three hours. They were not, therefore, high-speed trains in the current meaning of that term. But the later RTG, which was of five cars instead of four, and in which a second turbine replaced the diesel, has a maximum speed of 200 km/h (125 mph). The French were not the first to employ gas turbine power successfully. In the 1950s the Union Pacific Railroad introduced a series of gas turbine freight locomotives and in 1964 several US and Canadian railways bought an American-built turbo-train design which, however, proved somewhat unreliable in service. More recently, Amtrak has put into service new turbo trains of the French design.

The latest high-speed train service is that of the Western Region of British Rail, the former Great Western Railway. Its HST units, introduced in 1976, have transformed the services from London to Bristol and south Wales. They are diesel-electric train sets, with a power car at each end, and are designed for a maximum speed of 200 km/h (125 mph). They have brought the Bristol–London schedule down to 90 minutes for the 189 km (118 mile) journey, including one or two intermediate stops. These speeds have been sufficient to attract passengers from the parallel

Far left: One of the High Speed Trains (HST), capable of 200 km/h (125 mph), of the Western Region of British Rail. Left: A prototype British APT (Advanced Passenger Train). Above: In recent decades suburban services have been of great value to society but highly unprofitable for the railways, who have to make available rolling stock and trackage which is required only for four hours and on five days a week. Doubledeck trains can sometimes enable more passengers to be carried without investing in extra tracks or longer stations. This is a modern French example, one of several which entered Paris commuter service in 1975.

motorway and, additionally, to provide British Rail with the favourable publicity which it attracts all too rarely. In 1977, to celebrate the Silver Jubilee, an HST was run from Bristol to London in just 70 minutes, representing an average of 165 km/h (103 mph).

The success of the HST made it appear doubtful whether British Rail's next step, the Advanced Passenger Train (APT), was really worthwhile. This technologically very advanced project incorporates a tilting mechanism to enable it to travel at high speed over existing curves without discomfort for passengers. But it is very expensive, and the spending of many millions of pounds to obtain just a few minutes improvement over HST timings seems hard to justify.

Tilting body high-speed trains are also under development elsewhere. The Canadian LRC is the nearest to regular service. This differs from the APT in that only the cars, not the locomotives, have a tilting capacity, and the locomotives themselves are true locomotives, not power cars; this means that the LRC is readily re-marshalled into a longer or shorter train. Tilting bodies are also being studied in Sweden, Spain, Italy, France, Germany and elsewhere.

Japan's New Tokaido Line is an example of the high-speed railway, as opposed to the high-speed train. Although the Tokaido Line will not be expanded into as large a network as was originally hoped, the concept of the high-speed railway has now been adopted by several other countries. In Germany, by reconstructing existing main lines and building some entirely new mileage, high-speed routes are being created between Hanover and Würzburg and between Mannheim and Stuttgart. As early as 1965, to mark a transport exhibition at Munich, the German Railways introduced a regular 200 km/h (125 mph) schedule between Augsburg and Munich, but this did not last long because of unexpected wear and tear to both track and rolling stock. Although this service was reinstated in 1977 the German Railways envisage that the trains on the new high-speed lines of the 1980s, on which speeds of up to 300 km/h (185 mph) are expected, will be lightweight electric multiple unit trains similar to the ET 403 type.

The most spectacular of the European high-speed railways will almost certainly be France's Paris-Sudest line. Ostensibly planned to relieve the pressure on the existing Paris–Lyons main line, the new railway is evidently a prestige endeavour designed to restore France to the leading position in railway technology. It is a completely new line, leaving the existing railway 28 km (17 miles) from Paris and rejoining it just north of Lyons. It will be 390 km (242 miles) long, and will come into service in 1980. Originally it had been intended to use a new generation of fast turbotrains on this route but, perhaps

because of the high fuel consumption of the latter, it was finally decided to use electrification. Electric multiple-unit trains, rather similar to the superseded turbotrain prototype, will be permitted to run at up to 260 km/h (161 mph), thereby reducing the Paris–Lyons schedule to just two hours. Such an acceleration will also benefit services which will use the new route for part of their run. Geneva, for example, will be brought within three and a half hours of Paris. It is claimed that the new line will carry 15 million passengers annually, and that the investment will be recouped within ten years. Even allowing for the traditional optimism of railway promoters, it seems likely that the line will be commercially successful, provided that current travel trends are maintained. After all, about one third of the French population will be within easy reach of the line. So confident are the predictions that there is already a second project under consideration by the SNCF: the Paris–Nordouest from Paris to Nantes and Brest. This line, however, would make great use of existing, but reconstructed, line.

Top: The French TGV prototype, a high-speed gas turbine train. Similar trains, but electrically powered, will be used on the new Sud Est Line. Far left: One of the earlier French post-war electric locomotives. Above left: A modern example of the French 'autorails', diesel railcars which since the 1930s have taken over most of the French secondary passenger services. Above: A New Zealand example of the electric multiple unit suburban train. Below: One of the British 'Deltic' locomotives.

Left: A series of new or upgraded main lines was approved for Germany in 1973 which would permit speeds of 300 km/h (185 mph) or faster, and work soon started on the first such link, between Hanover and Kassel. The ET 403 is a high-speed multiple unit intended as a prototype of the trains which will use these new routes.

Freight trains after steam

Most of the world's railways obtain more revenue from freight than from passenger traffic. The exceptions are a few mainly-commuter railways, like the Long Island Railroad in America and the Southern Region of British Rail, together with a handful of systems which, like the Netherlands Railways, face unfavourable geographical conditions for freight movement. Few railways ever had a complete monopoly of freight transport. In their early decades they fought with the inland waterways for traffic, but only in Britain was their victory near complete; at present, apart from the Netherlands Railways, the American and German railways are among those which lose much potential traffic to the rivers and canals.

However, it was the coming of the motor truck which after several decades brought the railways to a state of financial crisis. During World War 1 many vehicles had been built for military needs, and when the war finished thousands of unwanted vehicles were sold off cheaply. Since the armies had also trained soldiers to drive these trucks there was a large pool of drivers among the newly-demobilized armies. Some ex-soldiers set themselves up as one-man trucking enterprises, while others joined the few early large-scale road transport firms.

For a number of reasons, the railways were highly vulnerable to this new competition. By this time most of them had freight-rate structures with a high element of cross-subsidization; that is, high charges levied on some types of freight, or in some areas, were used to compensate for low rates charged elsewhere. Although much of this cross-subsidization had arisen when railway companies had tried to undercut rates on traffic for which several companies competed, making up their losses on traffic which was safely in their hands, there was a social justification for this kind of discrimination. The railways were treated legally as common carriers, required to handle any traffic that

Left: A mixed freight train of the New York Central (now part of Conrail) crosses the Mohawk River at Pattersonville, N.Y., hauled by three General Motors diesel units.

was offered, including much traffic from impoverished industries or impoverished areas which could never be profitable and had to be balanced by higher charges elsewhere. In general, throughout the world, railways fixed their rates on a 'what the traffic will bear' principle, which meant that expensive items like manufactured products paid much higher rates than cheap products like grain or coal. This meant that a road transport enterprise could easily undercut the railway rate on high-value freight and still make a handsome profit.

To this tactical advantage in charging, the trucker could also add, in most cases, a better service. It took decades for railway administrators to realize (some still do not realize) that a railway's customers are not impressed by ever-increasing train loads or even by ever-increasing maximum speeds. What they are interested in is the time taken from the senders' gate to the receiver's door. Traditionally, railway freight was first taken to the freight station, loaded into a freight car which was then held until the next freight train took it to a big marshalling yard where it would again wait until enough cars moving in the same direction had accumulated to form a train. The resulting long transit time was not serious for cheap bulk goods, but it was disliked by shippers of the more-highly-valued freight, who soon turned to the truck operator. A truckload of freight would travel directly from door to door, and would not wait for hours while other loads were accumulated. In the 1920s the trucker who promised 'next morning delivery' had a great advantage over the competing railway.

But governments, or at least most governments, realized that this situation could drive the railroads out of business, and then there would be no transport for the cheaper-value but essential traffic. From the social point of view, therefore, the railways had to be helped. The amount of such help varied in each country. In some, including Germany and France, restrictions were placed on the new trucking companies. In Britain and America the railways agitated for legislation to limit trucking, but with little success.

Above: The heaviest unit trains on the 1067 mm (3 ft 6 in) gauge are operated by the Queensland Railways in Australia. Two English Electric diesel locomotives haul a 4500-tonne bauxite train to the refineries at Kwinana.

Left: Overhead gantries, although expensive, have been found by several railways, including the French, to be the best means of moving containers between rail and road vehicles.

Right: Freight cars with sliding roofs in SNCF service.

In Britain there was some such legislation, but it was not strictly applied. For example, while the British railways were strictly required to observe limitations on the number of hours worked by their employees, the road transport companies ignored (and some still ignore) these regulations. However, in Britain there was a partial success in securing bigger licence fees for motor trucks. After all, argued the railways, about one-fifth of railway costs are accounted for by track and signalling, which are provided from the railways' own resources whereas the motor truck uses (and wears out) roads paid for by the taxpayer.

In Britain freight traffic has declined absolutely since the peak of 1923, with a temporary resurgence during World War II. In the USA and Canada, parts of western Europe, and Australasia, the decline has not been absolute but only proportional, with the railways carrying more freight but a declining share of the total traffic, and often with an absolute loss in the more profitable categories. In Russia and the other planned economies the railways have carried ever-increasing loads because of the rapid development of heavy industry and the strict limitation of road transport. Indeed, the USSR carries one-half of the world's total railway freight traffic.

Loss of freight to the highways has been particularly serious in North America, where even the cheap bulk traffic for which railways are technically best suited have been threatened. A truck which carries high-value goods in one direction can advantageously carry low-rated freight on the return trip, for it is better to carry freight at a loss than to carry no freight at all. In general American railway managements have been very slow to adjust themselves to the new competition, and to abandon their take-it-or-leave-it attitude towards their clients. They have preferred to pin their faith in innovations like the diesel locomotive, which postponed rather than eliminated the day of reckoning. It must be admitted, however, that those railway managements which did try to compete were discouraged by unfair treatment. On several occasions, for example, a railroad which, by new technology such as larger freight cars, reduced its costs was not allowed by the Interstate Commerce Commission to lower its rates to match; such lowering of charges was hypocritically termed 'unfair competition'.

To the American railroader the diesel-electric locomotive nevertheless seemed to be one of those new technologies which, by reducing operating costs, would ultimately enable the railways to offer charges below those which the high-cost truck operator could charge. Although the capital cost of a diesel was two or three times higher than that of a steam locomotive, its running costs were lower. Moreover, a fireman

Left: One of the new generation of yards—the Canadian Pacific's Alyth yard near Calgary. Below: Four diesel units haul a transcontinental train of boxcars through the Rockies in California. At this point, Feather River Canyon, the railway spirals over bridges and through tunnels to gain height.

Above: Two Canadian Pacific diesel units haul a freight through wild Ontario terrain near Port Coldwell.

would no longer be necessary, so that the most expensive item of labour cost, the highly-paid loco-motive crew, would be significantly reduced. How-ever, when the US railroads had completed their dieselization programmes these advantages had failed to materialize. The railroads were heavily in debt; having scrapped new and undepreciated steam loco-motives they had contracted enormous bank loans to pay for their diesels. A nationwide strike and political muscle had enabled the locomotive mens' union to insist that firemen would still be carried by diesel locomotives (and 'full-crew' laws in many states meant that a minimum of five workers were required to move even a locomotive by itself). What the diesel did do, however, was enable the railroads to offer faster train services. These were particularly advan-tageous on the longer runs, where delays in marshal-ling yards were proportionately less serious. Even so, the trains had to move fast to compete with the 'double-bottom rig', the truck-plus-trailer combina-tion with two-man crew and bunk for the off-duty driver, which speeded along the new Trans-America

Above: Two diesel units of the New South Wales Railways with a bulk freight train. Below left: A freight train of the New York Central between Buffalo and Albany.

highways. By the early 1970s the Santa Fe Railroad's *Super C* was the world's fastest freight train, on one 328 km (205 mile) sector of its transcontinental run averaging 112 km/h (70 mph). Other fast American freights included the Southern Pacific's *Blue Streak Merchandise* and the Union Pacific's *Overland Mail*, both of which averaged more than 110 km/h (65 mph) for parts of their trip. Such speeds were matched by a few European freights, designed to meet similar highway competition. In France the *Provence Express*, operated from the south to Paris in the fruit season, and the *Mediterranée Frêt*, both averaged more than 96 km/h (60 mph), as did several of British Rail's *Freightliners* on the electrified London to Crewe line.

Fast freight trains were not a new product of the diesel age, however. The mail and newspaper trains operated by many railways well before World War 1 were forerunners, and in the inter-war period, to meet highway competition, many companies introduced the express freight. In America the first such train was the Cotton Belt Railroad's *Blue Streak* of 1931 which was the world's fastest freight train and which offered morning-after delivery for freight from St Louis to Arkansas. In Britain the fast parcels train was multiplied, carrying high-value freight in less-than-carload consignments. The British railways, together with the Russian, were also early users of the container, a mode of transport which would not be exploited in most countries until recent decades.

The container was essentially a large box, at first wooden, with end doors. It could be transferred by a small crane from railway flat car to flat-bed motor truck in minutes. Consignments could therefore be loaded into the container at a shipper's premises, and taken by truck to the railway where the container was loaded on a flat car for the trunk element of its trip. On arrival, another truck would take the container to its final destination. In this way the railway could offer the same door-to-door service as the trucker. In Russia, where truck competition did not exist, the container still had a technical appeal, as it eliminated the transhipment of freight between truck and train which was time-consuming, costly, and subject to pilferage and damage.

After World War II, when road competition was even more crippling, other railway systems adopted the container idea, or its half-brother, the trailer-on-flatcar ('piggyback'). The latter was the carrying on flat cars of an entire road vehicle, complete with wheels. By this time much long-distance road haulage was carried out with large semi-trailers hauled by a tractor unit. At the new 'piggyback' terminals semi-trailers were detachable from their tractors and loaded on to railway flat cars. The French and American railways at first favoured this mode. The semi-trailer, unlike the container, was equipment already very familiar to trucking companies and to shippers, who would soon realize that by using rail for the mainline segment of the haul they would dispense with the expensive tractor unit and its driver for all but the pick-up and delivery segment. Most railways offering 'piggyback' not only established fleets of tractors and

trailers but also encouraged their former rivals, the truck companies, to use the service with their own trailers, as well as industries hitherto operating private trailers.

The disadvantage of 'piggyback' was that it required high clearances above the railway track, although the French solved this problem with their 'Kangaroo' flatcars in which the wheels of the semi-trailer were lowered into a pocket beneath the floor of the flat car. In Britain, with its very restricted clearances, 'piggyback' was not favoured. In the USA the division of the railroad network between a host of independent companies resulted in the development of competing systems of 'piggyback' and containers

Above left: The cattle train still thrives in Queensland. Left: New Zealand Railways, like British Rail, still uses many small 4-wheel freight cars. Above: Assembling a new US diesel locomotive.

which were not interchangeable, so that a given container or trailer could be routed only to those railroads which had chosen the same system. The main division was between those lines which had chosen 'piggyback' and those which had preferred containers; with 'piggyback', it was argued, the railroads were transporting about the country beneath the semi-trailers hundreds of unwanted pairs of wheels. Among the container operators, different methods of transferring the container between flat-bed truck and railway flat car were used. Some preferred cranes, and others one of the several methods for sliding the container off and on. Each method required its own non-interchangeable design of container and flat car. With 'piggyback' there were similar conflicts between different tie-down methods. Thus even now there is a lack of standardization between US railroads in this field, and this has hampered the full exploitation of the new technology.

However, ocean shipping companies have been better coordinated, and their insistence on standard dimensions for containers in international service has meant an increasing number of US railroads both willing and able to provide facilities for these standard containers, interchanged between land and sea.

The rail–sea interchange of containers has developed rapidly since the 1960s. It is now possible to send containers from Britain via Russia to the Pacific, for shipment to Japan; this takes several weeks less than the traditional all-sea transit. In the early 1970s international shipping companies persuaded the Penn-Central and Santa Fe railroads to begin the 'land bridge' service across the USA. Containers from Europe to California or Japan, and from the Eastern states to Japan, were sent by rail across America instead of moving by sea via the Panama Canal. At Richmond, California, those containers destined for Japan were reloaded on to container ships. The corresponding eastern terminal was at Weehawken in New Jersey, and the 60-car trains were allowed five days to cross the continent.

Although the temporary abandonment of the Channel Tunnel project in 1975 was a setback to plans for further integration of long-distance freight services throughout Europe, moves towards commercial and technical coordination continued. Such cooperation is long established, and several international railway organizations existed long before European economic integration was thought of. The International Union of Railways (UIC) has done much valuable work: freight car parameters of the European railways are largely standardized, and there is a European freight car pool to regulate the movement of vehicles over foreign systems. Current developments at the UIC include the design of twelve freight-car types destined to be the standards for the western European railways. However, the ambitious intention of equipping all cars with automatic couplings by 1980 has been deferred. In eastern Europe there have recently been similar developments, although the situation there is complicated by the different gauge of the Soviet railways; although passenger cars change their wheelsets at the frontier, Russian freight cars remain on their own territory.

Another organization linking most European railways is Intercontainer, which is a coordinating agency for the various railways' international container services. Such cooperation between railways can provide better utilization of containers (in particular by obtaining a return load) and also offer a more complete service to clients. Trans-European container trains have been a logical further step, and seem likely to develop well beyond the early Paris–Cologne and Paris–Rotterdam services. For international non-container trains, there is the TEEM network of fast freight services. Another organization, now approaching its thirtieth birthday, is Interfrigo, which handles the international refrigerator car services of the continental railways. One of its best-known services are the refrigerator trains conveying Spanish fruit to northern Europe, and consisting of vehicles which have their wheelsets changed to enable them to run over the Spanish broad gauge.

The modern high-speed container train has perhaps been most fully exploited in Britain, where container-only Freightliner trains run over the main routes between terminals equipped with special gantry cranes for quick transhipment between rail and road vehicles. Although some of the more optimistic predictions made in the 1950s have not been fulfilled, with some newly established container services failing to attract much business, in general the technique has retained, and even regained, for British Rail much high-value merchandise traffic. Like other nationalized and highly centralized railways, British Rail has not been plagued with a multiplicity of uncoordinated container systems; it chose what it considered to be the best, and stuck to its choice, with obvious benefits.

Containers were the ideal medium for fairly small consignments of high-value goods for which prompt delivery and elimination of reloading en route were important. Traditional bulk commodities for which rail transport, with its ability to move thousands of tonnes with just one train crew, is most suitable require a different technique. Here the capacity to increase train loads is the most important cost-reducing factor.

With electric and diesel power, where tractive effort can be readily increased simply by adding additional locomotive units, the limit to train load is now the length of passing loops and the strength of car couplings. To a large extent the latter limitation can be circumvented by placing some of the locomotive units in the centre or towards the rear of long trains. Such units are controlled by radio by the locomotive crew in the leading unit. The first examples of this kind of operation were in the USA, but the technique is now spreading. It is connected with the increasing importance of the 'unit-train' concept. This is not a new idea, but is now being exploited more thoroughly. It implies the operation of trains carrying a single commodity from a single origin to a single destination. By eliminating intermediate marshalling, this significantly reduces the time and cost of the shipment. A modern and technically advanced example is the 'Merry-go-round' system of British Rail. In this, trains of fixed formation circulate between particular collieries and power stations in what is technically a never-stop process, for the specially designed coal cars are loaded and unloaded while still moving at a very low speed. Thus the expensive locomotives and cars are intensively utilized, unlike the stock used in traditional freight service. A similar operation, using rather bigger locomotives and cars is that of the 125 km (78 mile) Black Mesa and Lake Powell line in Arizona. This is a non-common-carrier line, an echo of the private colliery railways of the dawn of railways. It conveys coal to a giant power station, deriving current at 50,000 volts to power its locomotives. More recently, a method of discharging oil from trains on the move has been developed in Canada, and oil is now sent by Merry-go-round train to the power station at Lennox in Quebec. Another type of unit train used especially in Britain, is the 'Company Train', made up of the client's own specialized rolling stock. Big industries, like oil companies, use these trains in regular services to distribute specialized products between their main centres.

Left: Five diesel units are needed to haul this Denver and Rio Grande freight train through the Tennessee Pass in Colorado.

Index

Page numbers in italics refer to illustration captions.

ACKNOWLEDGMENTS

The publishers would like to thank the following organisations and individuals for their kind permission to reproduce the photographs in this book:

W.J.V. Andersen 32–33, 36–37, 59 below; ANP Photo 74–75; Australian Information Service, London 76 right, 77; R. Bastin 79; F.J. Bellwood 11 above left and below, 76 above; Yves Broncard 87 centre left; Canadian Pacific 95 above, 96–97; C.C.Q. 31 above, (T.B. Owen) 78 above; J.A. Coiley 68 centre; Colourview Picture Library, (P.B. Whitehouse) 53; Deutsches Bundesbahn 88–89; F.P.G. 72 centre, 101; C.J. Gammell 12, 30, 31 below, 38 right, 50–51, 54, 55, 60 above and below, 62, 68 above; V. Goldberg 22–23; Victor Hand 20, 27 above, 28, 29, 35, 40 above and below, 42, 43, 44–45, 46–47, 48 above and below, 49 above and below, 52, 66–67, 70, 71 above and below, 90, 95 below, 98 below, 102; Government of India Tourist Office 84; Interfoto 39 right; Jim Jarvis 16 above, 18–19, 24–25, 59 above; D. Jenkinson 63 below, 83; Richard Kindig 21 above and below, 26, 27 below, 56–57, 58; London Transport 13 above; Merseyside County Museums 11 above right; Andrew Morland 16 centre; New Zealand Railways 76 left, 87 centre right, 100 below; L.A. Nixon 69 above and below; Picturepoint contents; F.L. Pugh 64; Rapho Agence de Presse 81; Railways of Australia 92–93, 98–99, 100 above; Science Museum 6, 8, 9, 14–15; S.N.C.F. 72 below, 80 below, 82 above and below, 85 above, (Lamber) 86–87 above, (Mazo) 94 right; Brian Stephenson 34 above, 80 above, 86 centre; Stock colour International 78 below; P.N. Trotter end papers, title, 65, 87 below; La Vie du Rail 13 centre, 34 centre, 80 centre; J.N. Westwood 73; J.S. Whiteley 63 above; D. Wilkinson 38 left.